The Idea Is...

A book for turning ideas into companies

Matt Paulin

Version 1.0.0

Copyright © 2014 Matt Paulin

All rights reserved.

ISBN: 1494482827
ISBN-13: 978-1494482824

For Tessa and Lucas

Table of Contents

Introduction... vi

Change Log... x

Ideation... 11

Chapter 1: Creating Ideas..12

Chapter 2: Group Ideation...29

Chapter 3: DIY Think Tank..41

Chapter 4: Judging Ideas..59

Incubation..80

Chapter 5: Ideas into Businesses...81

Chapter 6: The Incubation Process..89

Chapter 7: The Vision and the Charter...103

Chapter 8: The Life of an Idea..127

Chapter 9: Including Investment..138

Chapter 10: Putting it all together...144

Formation...153

Chapter 11: Accounting for Effort...154

Chapter 12: Ownership 166

Chapter 13: Structural Recipes...175

Chapter 14: Company Formation..193

Chapter 15: Goodbye!... 201

Acknowledgements.. 203

About the Author..205

Further Reading... 206

Introduction

Where do businesses come from? This is the question that has been the focus of the last decade of my life. Living in the modern world means interacting with businesses: you trade with them, most likely have worked for and invested in at least one, and you may even hope to own your own someday. They're everywhere, but they all started somewhere. I am fascinated by how these social constructs, which touch nearly everyone's life in one form or another, take shape.

I call them social constructs, not just legal ones, because underneath all of that paperwork and accounting is a very emotional world. They form the setting for amazingly complex and dynamic social dances that we all go through. Businesses are comprised of real people with dreams and aspirations.

Most businesses are the product of a team rather than of one person. Even the one-man or one-woman consulting businesses depend on accountants and other service providers who influence them. Businesses are built around trade with other people, and as such, they are inherently social; you must communicate well to run one effectively.

What really fascinates me is the beginning stage of a business, when those dreams and aspirations first come together to form something. At one point in time, a company doesn't exist, and then all of a sudden it does. Certain events led up to the founding moment, and later decisions were made that influence the culture of that business forever.

The real crux for me is that somewhere in here an idea formed. This is amazing by itself, but what is even more amazing is when that idea grows and people congregate around it, and over time, that idea turns into a business.

Taking an idea and turning it into a company is extremely difficult.

After the idea comes a critical transition phase. This is the make-or-break stage; what should happen here? This book will focus on answering exactly that question, but it will do so by examining the *social* challenges of such transitions.

In 2005 I founded the software engineering firm, PugetWorks. Through PugetWorks my team and I have been contracted on hundreds of software projects where more than thirty were start-up companies. This was an excellent chance to see all the different dynamics at play in the formation and growth of new companies. PugetWorks wasn't intended to be just a software engineering firm, but a incubator where we have created six companies of our own. This book is a collection of the lessons learned and an overarching way to make sense of it all.

The following is the book's roadmap and tells the story of what formed from this adventure. It will guide you through the next set of chapters as we discuss each of these different parts.

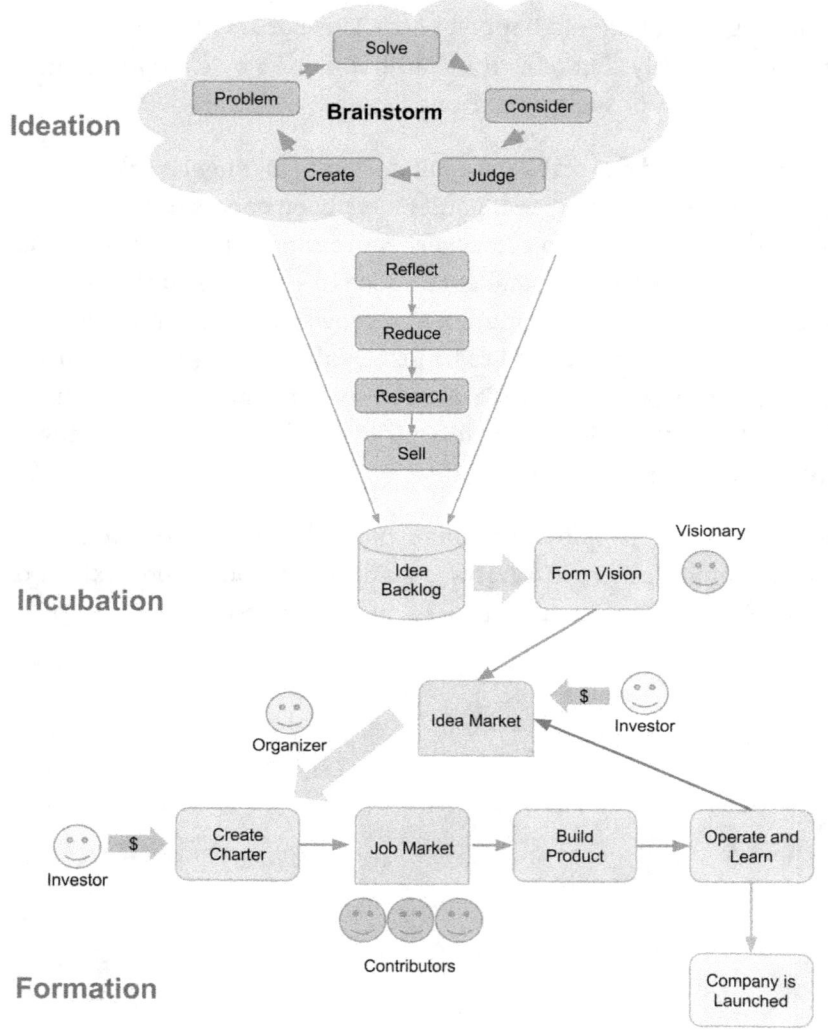

Ultimately this process will help you to bridge the gap from dreaming up an idea to turning it into a company. The end result is a structure that can be applied to groups of people just starting out - or even within existing companies - for the sole purpose of building out ideas. It is general-purpose enough that it can even be applied to ventures that aren't for-profit companies *per se*; in other words, it can be useful to any collective of people looking to Get Something Done.

I will be taking you on a journey where we start by looking at how an idea forms. I will show you a process that we are using and improving upon every day in the real world to spawn new businesses. For the most part, this process was designed to address the problems that naturally happen when people take on a mutual risk to seize an opportunity. PugetWorks, has been play-testing this process for a long time, and it has become more effective with each iteration. Turning ideas into companies is a very difficult skill to acquire, and I could only hope that this book helps you along this path.

Lastly, I want to point out that I do not know everything on this subject. This book will be a continuous work in progress. To keep it organized I have added a change log which will explain what has been added since the last versions.

Change Log

Version 1.0.0 : January 23, 2014: First release.

Ideation

It all starts here. In this first section of the book we will talk about how ideas form and how to get more of them.

Chapter 1: Creating Ideas

Think about an idea you came up with. It might have been an old one or something you just thought of. At one time it didn't exist, and then, "Pop!" It just ended up in your mind.

How does that happen? Where does it come from? How can you make this happen more often? This chapter explores answers to these three questions.

The following chapter will help you to come up with ideas by first considering their origins. It establishes a vocabulary for talking about ideas and what is transpiring in our minds when we try to solve problems. Let's start by considering the conscious and subconscious parts of our minds.

The Ideas in the back of your mind.

Good ideas don't come out of nowhere. Most likely, you've been thinking about them for a long time. They often begin as interests we keep coming back to again and again. Maybe an idea comes from something that makes you angry, and you know that there is a better way to do it. Maybe it's a particular technology you keep trying to apply as a fix to an unrelated problem. It could just be a group of people whom you want to help. Whatever the driving motivation, there is certainly a phenomenon in our minds where we harbor a certain set of ideas that define us.

In our subconscious these fragments bounce around and mingle. When something sparks that interest again, they fire up. They start to glom together and every so often a fully formed idea emerges. The following diagram is the best way I can think of to describe this:

Ideation

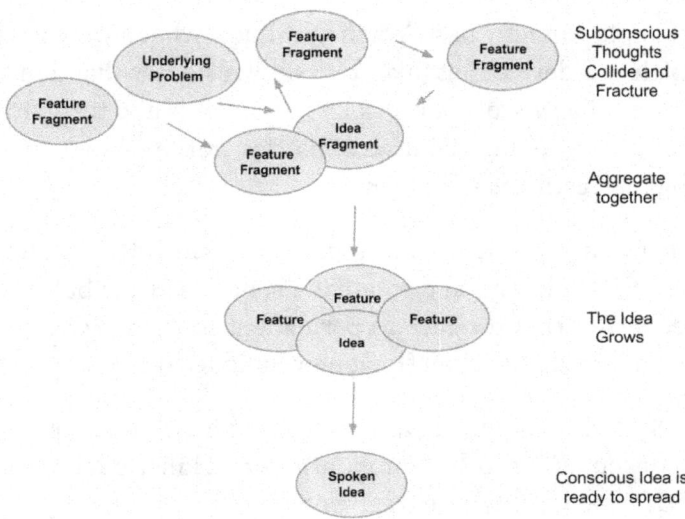

Fragments: There is a period before the ideas existed. It's more of a period where you are interested in a subject. You are attracted to information about this subject on a more informational level. Maybe you saw some sort of technological work, or work of art, and were inspired. Maybe you learned of a bad situation and dwelled on how best to help. It is a period where you have a strong emotion. That emotion creates a sort of 'collector' in your mind. Information and passing thoughts on the subject start to collect together in this place. An important thing to remember is that this process is emotional - very emotional, in fact and that is what is driving the process. If you didn't care, these fragments would simply not gather themselves.

Aggregation: This period is characterized by the aforementioned fragments bouncing around, being added to, and activating. Your mind gets stimulated and the same fragments light up over and over. Then you encounter another subject. At some point there is a connection. That is when the idea happens. Now when you think of one subject, it will forever be connected to another subject by an idea.

Here is an example from my past: You might know what a *wave bottle* is. A wave bottle is a device that takes two similar liquids that don't mix but have a similar viscosity, typically mineral oils and turpentine. I once got on a kick thinking about wave bottles; at the same time I was exploring interesting wall hangings.

Then, one day I came up with an idea to put the wave bottle in a huge petri dish, mount it sideways and rotate it. From this idea, I built a wall-mounted device that produced a permanent standing wave on my wall. The end result was something new, unique, and fun.

Before the idea itself, though, I had two idea fragments, one for the wave bottle concept and another for paintings and kinetic sculpture. The idea then formed from these fragments.

Growing period: Now an idea exists in your head. It will start to grow and you will periodically re-evaluate it. It is enough of an idea that you can call it to the front of your mind. But it isn't so strong that you feel compelled to talk about it. It's more of a toy for you to play with in your head, something amusing, a type of diversion. Maybe you repress it, thinking it a waste of time or too ambitious - thus filtering it out of your focus so that you can do what you are supposed to do.

However, as long as you can see the problem that this idea would solve, that idea won't leave you alone. It comes back from time to time and you might add to it here or there. Slowly, the idea wins you over as something useful and possible.

An idea: Finally, if the idea seems to be worth talking about, maybe you will write it down, or maybe you will tell someone about it. In terms of forming an idea, this represents success. It has to be created and communicated. If the idea is interesting, it might be read or repeated by someone else. If it is badly communicated it might mutate or never jump the gap into someone else's mind.

Sources for idea

If you know a source of ideas then you know where to look for innovation. From interviewing people with big ideas and members of our idea community, and from my own personal experience, I have found that ideas do come from distinct sources. This may not be a complete list, but it should help you pay attention to certain situations when you are looking for new ideas.

Ideas from directed problem solving

It all starts with the thought, "There must be a better way." Then your mind races through its experiences, tricks, and whatever else can light up in your brain. Out the other side comes a solution.

I think this is the most common source of ideas. It is the most repeatable and at least you know you will get a result. It seems that companies go through this loop constantly. They survey or study what is wrong with products and then solve those problems. It is an iterative approach to figuring out what to do next and it's probably the easiest type of idea to judge.

Ideas from playing

You find something on your desk, perhaps a paperclip, and the thought "what can I do with this?" pops into your head. Maybe you unbend it and make a little person, or a tiny bow and arrow. A piece of tape turns it into a flag. As you continue to play with these items, your mind can relax and refocus. What comes out are the more whimsical, fun ideas. This is great practice for keeping your mind limber for when you need to come up with a more serious idea. And it is very easy to do. Pick any object near you and try to think of all the things you could use it for. A few ideas will come to mind.

Ideas from miscommunication

I love it when this happens but it is absolutely unpredictable. Maybe you have had this experience: You walk up to a friend and tell him your idea for solving a problem. It's complex, the friend is not paying attention, and he hears something different from what you intended to say. He doesn't quite understand but tries to figure out what you are talking about. A debate ensues. After several minutes, you both realize that neither one of you was on the same page, but the idea that results from the discussion is much better than the one you started with. Neither person truly was the source of the idea. But both of you walk away amazed at the results.

Ideas from a change in resources

When a new technology or cheaper approach becomes available it can change the landscape of what is possible. Think about the music industry and the rise of computers. The music industry was built partially on the way the music was distributed. They could sell you a compact disc at a huge markup to cover what the CD cost to manufacture. Then, in the 90's computer technology grew rapidly and songs could easily be copied, eliminating the need for the CD itself.

Suddenly, the music industry was hit by a wave of technology that altered the fundamental item they had been selling. The same sort of thing happens in any industry when an assumed constant suddenly changes. Anywhere you discover that a resource is about to change price automatically becomes a good place to look for innovation.

Ideas from research

Imagine you are grinding your way through the scientific process: gathering data, proving or disproving a hypothesis, and hoping to learn more in the process.

Then, something really strange happens: You get results that were totally unexpected. You run the experiment again; same results. You realize you were asking the wrong questions to begin with, but as you learn more about what you are seeing you start to realize just what the implications are. A flood of ideas comes into your mind because you've noticed something no one else is aware of.

These epiphanies didn't come from solving a problem, but from realizing what is now possible. These are my favorite ideas because they were always right in front of us, we were just blind to the possibilities until our perspective changed.

Ideas from competition.

This is similar to ideas from research in that a belief is shattered, in this case not from studying the world around you, but from the inspiration of seeing someone else do it first.

One of my favorite periods of history is the Cold War 'space race.' The space program was not so much about putting people in space as about the competition between the U.S. and the Soviet Union for prestige. First, no one thought it possible to achieve orbit, then they didn't think you could do a high orbit, then they didn't think you could get to the moon. Each preconception was summarily shattered, and seemingly intractable problems were solved almost overnight. The competition between these countries changed their expectations of what was possible.

Ideas from zoning out.

Unfocused daydreaming gives the visual side of the mind a chance to find patterns and to make connections between seemingly unconnected ideas. If a mind is stressed, worried, and over-focused, when it stops focusing too intently it might just start making connections between things that it never has before.

August Kekule, the French chemist, was trying to disprove the belief that the structures of atoms were "unknowable". He was focused on figuring out the curious fact that the chemical benzene has a 1:1 carbon hydrogen ratio. He had focused on this problem for years. Then one day he began dozing off and had what he described as a "waking dream". In his vision he saw a snake biting its own tail. When he awoke he realized that this was his subconscious mind telling him that carbon atoms could form into a ring. From this he described the shape of benzene as a ring of atoms.

How Ideas Strengthen

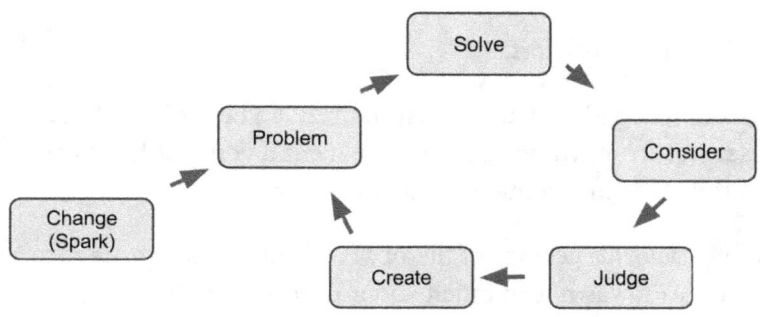

1. **Change:** You are doing something on a new subject, new place, new people. This is what sparks the cycle.

2. **Problem:** You notice that something isn't working as it should.

3. **Solve:** You have an idea for how to solve it.

4. **Consider:** Think of other problems implied by your solution, or alternative solutions

5. **Judge:** Decide if it is worth it after the glow wears off

6. **Create:** Build the idea, try to use it. Now go back to 2.

At any point along this path the idea might have been abandoned. It depends on the nature of the person and how much interest they have in what they are solving. The really interesting thing is that a single trip through this cycle could span years. We could be harboring hundreds of these ideas growing in us. Every time we encounter the subject again, we get re-energized and add more complexities to what we are trying to solve.

One thing to point out is that the amount of time we spend on the idea depends on the size of the problem we are trying to solve. For instance, if you are trying to figure out what to eat for dinner, then there's really not much at stake. On the other hand, if you are looking to solve world hunger then this will clearly require a bit more brilliance.

Communicating an Idea

Before we can really get to the heart of ideation we first need a common vocabulary. The word *idea* is tremendously overloaded and it would be best if I explain what I mean by it.

An idea is a special kind of thought that makes a connection between two bodies of knowledge that did not exist before. For my purposes, I'm going to pose that an idea consists of a name and a description of a couple sentences in length. It needs merely to spark the imagination of whomever is told the idea and to convey the gist of the originator's thought process.

There are several reason to adopt this definition for this book. One is that it distills the idea down to its very essence, making it easier to explain and understand. If the idea is hidden in several pages or badly communicated then it can be impossible to evaluate. By stating the idea with just a couple of sentences then you have to think about it as a sort of thirty-second elevator pitch. The name is merely a shortcut so that your friends will know what you are referring to later.

Keeping it short helps to prevent two or more ideas from getting mixed together. You can tease out the separate ideas and name them separately. One huge problem that I have seen is how ideas can glue together and confuse what is being communicated. It isn't that they are bad ideas; it is just that they have become unnecessarily intertwined. Once again by limiting its size to a couple of sentences you reduce the risk of getting several ideas lumped together.

Too often a miscommunication about an idea sends conversations down paths where it takes ten minutes for those involved to realize they were not even talking about the same thing. These couple of sentences should convey or at least limit the amount of miscommunication for communication's sake. Even if the idea is terrible, it is better to judge it for what it is than to end up in a confused argument defending an idea that wasn't yours to begin with.

The added benefit is that when your idea is reduced to such a small size, it is more easily judged. It's a lot easier to get your ego tied up in the idea if it is several pages long or spread out across several technologies. This is simply because you have put much more work into it. If you've spent all night working on something, you may feel more invested and less receptive to judgment. It's easy to see someone's honest reaction as a threat and feel compelled to defend your decisions. Keeping its description short makes it harder to feel ownership.

The final reason for this is purely pragmatic. Many ideation exercises require the idea to be written down on a note card. During idea generation, I have seen some really amusing note cards returned to me because I wasn't clear about this definition. Sometimes they are incoherent, sometimes they are just opinions. The idea itself needs to encapsulate a meaningful connection from the author, and to communicate that message to anyone who is reading it.

How can you improve your ideas?

In working with ideas and brainstorming groups I have noticed several useful habits that have helped me and others to come up with more ideas. The following tips are the results of those observations. These can be thought of more as habits that you can introduce into your life with the sole purpose of improving the ideas you come up with.

The question is "Why do we have problems coming up with ideas?" I would say that the following are the most common reasons why we don't come up with brilliant ideas every day.

- Staying focused

- Killing ideas too quickly.

- Remembering our ideas

- Falling in love with our ideas

- 'Feature Hoarding'

Problem 1: Staying Focused

Moving a subject to the front row of your mind.

There are always several thoughts going through our minds at the same time. Some of these thoughts hold our attention longer than others. I've noticed that I often have horrible control over which thoughts get the focus.

This is important, but it's something that can be improved with practiced. For instance, if you are at a point in your life when something must occupy your thoughts, like a significant other, a child, a relative, or a mortgage, then it doesn't really give you a lot of time to devote to your dreams. What you need to do is to find a reason to focus on the subjects that you would like to solve or explore further. What is so amazing about this is that you don't need to focus much to change your mind, just a little each day.

You don't need to become obsessed with a subject in your mind. But, you need to give it thought on a daily basis. Maybe that is just 5 minutes, maybe more. By revisiting a subject daily you will find yourself coming up with more residual ideas on the subject throughout the day. Here are a couple of activities that could help you in keeping these thoughts in the front row of your mind.

Tip 1: Writing

Writing is powerful. Not from the perspective of communication; you don't really ever have to show your writing to someone. Rather, it's powerful because it forces you to actually focus on the subject. It gets you to sort out all your thoughts on a topic and figure out how to clearly communicate it.

It helps even more when you think someone is going to read about it. So, blogging is great. Sure, you might have only two people read it, and one of them might be a bot from Google. But, you have to believe that when you put something online, someone out there is going to read it. So your mind is forced to focus. This is a handy trick.

Tip 2: Give a talk

Give a talk on your subject. Find a way to put together 20 slides and talk about your subject. Even if you are just giving the talk to your pets it still is a presentation and it will force you to think about it.

You have to focus, and what's even better is that you have to use your voice and your body language, you have to listen to the words, and you have to focus on communicating them to your audience. That's at least four sections of your brain working in tandem on the same subject.

When you talk you are using more parts of your brain than just your inner thoughts. Talking forces you to communicate, so you have to use the verbal part of your brain. Because you're listening to yourself, you also have another section of your brain filtering words back into thought. Then there is the really odd trick: giving a presentation forces you to move around. As you use hand gestures and your face to communicate on a subject you are stimulating parts of your brain in your brain stem. What all of this does is increase the odds that your brain will make new connections, and you will have a new insight into your subject. Conversation is powerful.

Tip 3: Put a reminder up

If you can find a picture of your subject, or just write the subject down somewhere visible where you find yourself thinking, you will think about the subject more. This is a very ambient way to keep reminding yourself about that subject. Remember the whole point is just to keep the subject in the front of your brain.

I think this is a key ingredient that is usually ignored. If you are confronted with a problem on a daily basis, you will start coming up with ways to solve it. Many people have ideas for businesses based on food, traffic, sleep, and homes because those things figure prominently in their lives.

It's those subjects and problems that we are visiting on a daily basis that are dictating what we are thinking about. To train yourself to think about an entirely different subject you need to surround yourself with that subject.

Problem 2: Killing ideas too quickly.

To be an adult you have to efficiently follow ideas that help you protect what is important to you. It's part of survival and it's a way of filtering out useless plans and pointless activities. It's just one of the stages of growing up that all we all enter at some point in our youth. But this behavior can kill off ideas before they have a chance to join to anything. So, the trick here is that you need to suppress your judgment of an idea for some period of time.

If you have kids or are ever around children you will know what I'm talking about. They don't judge when they are young. They have no idea what is realistic and what is not, what matters and doesn't matter. The astronaut could be flying his spaceship made of sand; in the next instant he could be wearing a cowboy hat. These thoughts don't seem silly to them; they are just channeling their imaginations. Children don't think about how a spaceship would fall apart or how the cowboy hat wouldn't fit in the space helmet. It just doesn't matter.

Tip 4: Solving Problems

Remember that ideas are really solutions to problems. You need practice solving these problems. But, where can you find a constant source of problems? Try the newspaper. If you read an article, start writing out what problems are identified in the article. There are always some. The more in-depth the article, the deeper the problems will be.

Tip 5: Write it down and judge it later.

It is an exercise to brainstorm and it forces you to simply write. You need to have a subject in mind. Start by focusing on the problems with this subject. As you think of the problems, maybe write them out: "The problem is...".

From that simple exercise, your mind will come up with a solution. Just write it down. Don't think about why the solution is silly, just plan to come back later and cross it out. You can always judge later. The only thing you need to make sure is that you have told yourself that no one else will ever read this. You will not be judged.

Tip 6: 30 minutes of creative license

If you come from a background of business all of this can be especially hard. Making fast decisions requires your mind to not waste time on silly ideas that are not going anywhere. But, for 30 minutes that is exactly what you need to brainstorm. You might not be able to withhold judgment for 30 minutes, but just start with 5 minutes and then work your way up from there. What you don't want to do is to immediately shoot your ideas down. Give them some room to breathe.

This may be a lot harder than you expect. So get an timer and brainstorm alone. As soon as you notice that you are judging the idea, ignore it and keep going. Don't kill the idea but, try to ignore the need to kill it.

Problem 3: Remembering our ideas

When it comes to ideas our memory can be our worst enemy. For me, I might have a great thought driving in the car, maybe I even obsess about it for half an hour. Then I find myself working on a different project, worrying about something, and hours later I remember that I was excited about something... but what?

Tip 7: Write it down

The solution to this is easy, write it down. Seriously, come up with some sort of system for keeping track of these little ideas. Text them to yourself, write it on scraps of paper in your wallet, carry a pad with you, just make sure they are going somewhere. Your system will evolve as you start to get more ideas and become used to the habit of tracking them.

We all have more ideas than we give ourselves credit for. Even if you are the type of person who says, "I never come up with anything," I do not believe you. Most likely you just don't remember what you came up with.

Problem 4: Falling in love with our ideas

This can be the most time-consuming problem regarding ideas. You have an idea, and your second thought is "I can't believe no one has ever thought of this before...". For the rest of the day you obsess about it. You notice how this idea could be the key to everything, how a billion-dollar business is just sitting there, out in the open, and nobody else has noticed it.

I think this happens to a lot of people. We have an idea and just go crazy thinking it is super-awesome and amazing. This is only a problem because we become blinded by our own amazingness. It might not be a great idea, or it might already have been done. But, it's important to evaluate it rationally.

Tip 8: Tell your friend

The best way to deal with this is to tell your significant other or friend about the idea - especially if that person happens to be a scientist or businessperson. These folks are wonderfully critical people. They will take some of the glow off the idea. The other thing to do is to write your idea down and wait three days. If it still seems super amazing, maybe it's time to do some research on the topic.

The bottom line is this: just because you have become infatuated with an idea doesn't make it a good one. Give it a little time to cool down in your mind, otherwise when you start to act on it you might ignore critical flaws in the idea simply because you are in love with it.

You can sometimes spot this behavior in others when they are told of a competing idea: rather than seeing the similarities to their own idea, they only nitpick the competitor's flaws. So the rule of thumb is: "You know when you are enamored with your own idea when you stop evaluating and instead defend it." Competitors should not make you defensive about your idea, they should help you refine it.

Problem 5: Feature Hoarding

Have you ever had someone tell you an idea and have no idea what they were talking about? Maybe it involved some other trendy new technology, but deep down inside, you didn't understand what problem the idea was trying to solve. It's very likely there was an idea in there somewhere, but so many features were added to it that it's hard to figure out what the original purpose was. I call this phenomenon feature hording and it tends to happen when someone has had an idea for too long.

This can happen to anyone; once you have an idea that you are enamored with, suddenly it can be used to solve everything. With every new problem, the idea is adapted to fit the situation by adding more technology and features. It seems that the longer someone has had the idea the more features it grows. Trim off some of those extra features with the following tip.

Tip 9: Explain the idea in 1 minute

In the simplest form the idea must be easy to communicate. If you find yourself explaining the idea for more than one minute, then you need to refine it.

Tell someone your idea. If you don't want to tell a person, stand in front of a mirror or your cat and tell it your idea. If you find yourself rambling for more than a minute, then start over again.

Keep trying this over and over until you have it down to one minute. Now write down in one sentence what the name of the idea is and a description. Then you can start to pull all the parts together into an organized state. Most likely you do have a good idea, but you might find you have have two or three instead.

We all have good ideas.

Ideas often come from two things coming together in a way they never did before. In an interview, the author Neil Gaiman was asked where his ideas come from. His response was the following:

> "'I make them up,' I tell them. 'Out of my head.' The ideas aren't the hard bit. They're a small component of the whole. Creating believable people who do more or less what you tell them to is much harder. And hardest by far is the process of simply sitting down and putting one word after another to construct whatever it is you're trying to build: making it interesting, making it new.
>
> You get ideas from daydreaming. You get ideas from being bored. You get ideas all the time. The only difference between writers and other people is we notice when we're doing it.
>
> You get ideas when you ask yourself simple questions. The most important of the questions is just, What if...?
>
> Another important question is, If only... I wonder... If this goes on... Wouldn't it be interesting if..." -- Neil Gaiman

The first step toward having more ideas is realizing that everyone has ideas and that yours are just as good as anyone else's. Start with a question in a topic you are interested in. Try out some of the tips in this chapter. Pretty soon you will notice that you have more of these ideas than you ever thought was possible.

Chapter 2: Group Ideation

Ideation is the process of generating, communicating, and developing new ideas. The key word here is 'process.' It isn't waiting for an idea to just pop out; it's an acknowledgement that to just get an idea requires preparation. How much time it takes to come up with that idea is dependent on many things, everything from what is going on around you to how much time you spend.

This problem isn't new. In 1953 Alex Osborn published the book *Applied Imagination*. Osborn worked in the advertising industry and was frustrated when his employees failed to come up with new ideas. So he started hosting group thinking sessions to help his employees become more creative. From his perspective, he was visualizing the team "storming" the problem like a squad of commandos. This is why we know this activity as "brainstorming".

A major part of brainstorming is to withhold criticism. Osborn wanted to create an environment of "freewheeling association". He believed that when people are too critical in their communication, the creativity of a group suffers. Instead of exploring bigger and more interesting ideas, his team would get stuck on the critiquing of a particular idea.

A key point was that Osborn focused on the quantity of ideas, not the quality of the ideas. He wanted people to switch into the mode of an explorer looking in every direction for what could be the next brilliant idea. In a similar vein you can see this same thinking in the third season of "Mad Men". The protagonist, Don Draper, asks his staff to "keep bringing me ideas to reject". He simply wants more ideas to choose from. This is a core arrangement in any creative group of people. The group is tasked with simply coming up with ideas. But the real decision-maker in such a group is someone we might call the *curator*. He or she looks through these ideas and finds the one with the right size and shape to fit the problem at hand. It's hard to do both parts well, but in this arrangement one person can simply come up with lots of ideas without over-thinking them. At the same time, another person can look at one idea after another searching for a good solution. This was Osborn's perspective as well; he just wanted lots of ideas. He felt he could always sort through them later. Quantity trumped quality any day.

Osborn also focused on recombining ideas, breaking down the different aspects and sticking them back together to form something new. Thus the idea was made up of many parts and by tweaking the idea you could rejoin it with other ideas to form something totally new.

The concept of "brainstorming" was a step forward in terms of how to come up with better ideas, but it did pose several problems such as criticism, teams, and ownership. Although they probably won't prevent you from coming up with ideas, they are known pitfalls you should be aware of when you design an effective brainstorming sessions.

Is Criticism Good?

Should you criticize an idea while you are brainstorming? The underlying assumption is that if people are scared to talk about their ideas, they will not talk. Thus fewer ideas will be produced. It turns out that this is fairly easy to test. You simply create a test group of subjects that come up with ideas individually and a second group that works as a team. Then count and rate the results.

Charlan Nemeth, a professor of psychology at the University of California at Berkeley, did just this in 2003. She gave 53 teams of five female undergraduates twenty minutes to brainstorm on the same problem. The catch was that one set of teams was instructed to debate, another set was instructed not to criticize, and the control group was given no instruction on how to organize.

The result was the team that involved debate and criticism came up with 20% more ideas than the other types of teams. One additional bonus was that the debate teams came up with an average of seven additional ideas after the session where the other teams only came up with three. Nemeth's team labeled these "residual ideas".

Why would the inclusion of criticism have this effect? I would argue that criticism isn't a filtering mechanism in itself. Rather, it's a way to get people to engage more deeply in the process. If you know that you have nothing to lose, you will create a lot of extra noise. But, if you know that you must defend something, or if you find yourself actually in a debate with another person, you will be forced to compete. I'm not talking about the 'bad' competition where there are winners and losers but rather the 'good' type of competition, where both opponents must become better simply to participate. This human interaction of debating makes the ideas stronger simply by forcing us to work harder to create them.

Take, for example, the game of poker. If you have ever played it with no money involved you will find yourself playing a very different game. People go "all in" early. Or they raise simply to do it. But if you make people put in five dollars, suddenly they take it seriously. Then it becomes a real game.

I think this analogy goes the same for ideation with one catch. It is important to get people warmed up and thinking creatively with the expectation that they will be defending these ideas later. So in my experience, having a brainstorming session first, then a filtering session afterward produces the best ideas.

Team or Alone?

The next question that tends to arise is "Should you brainstorm in a team, or by yourself?". Once again, fairly easy to test. You have people come up with ideas as individuals and then as a team. Judge the number of ideas and quality.

At Yale University in 1958, a research team did just this. This team had 48 men solve creative puzzles alone and 12 teams of four men solve puzzles as a team. The results were that the men working alone completed twice as many puzzles. The results from the individuals were even considered better solutions than the team. It appeared that the team brainstorming was giving people fewer and worse ideas.

There have been other studies similar to the one at Yale. Once you go down this path the next question is, why? Why are we less productive at coming up with ideas in groups? Michael Diehl and Wolfgang Stroebe, from Tubingen University in Germany, focused on this question. They isolated it down to the following five testable social phenomena:

1. *Free Riding*. This is the name of the situation where an individual feels their ideas are not worth as much when combined with others. In a group setting, participants don't feel like contributing their best ideas. Instead, they offer up only low-risk ideas in order to keep participating.

2. *Evaluation Apprehension*: Participants do not want to contribute because they believe their ideas will be judged harshly. Essentially, someone might not want to speak up and look foolish.

3. *Blocking*: Participants wait for other individuals to finish speaking and in the process forget what they were going to say.

4. *Social Matching Effects*: As humans we tend to match the amount of effort given by others on our team. In the case of brainstorming, an energetic team becomes increasingly more productive, whereas a calmer team tends to move more slowly. This is the energy of the team and it dictates how productive the team is.

5. *Illusion of Group Productivity*: There is a trend in group exercises to feel like more gets accomplished than actually does. When there is no obvious metric to determine success, the group's participants tend to be overly optimistic in their assessments of the group's performance. This in turn affects the ability of the group to come up with a large quantity of ideas. Similarly, individual group members tend to overestimate their own contributions.

The results of the study were intriguing. It turned out that Free Riding and Evaluation Apprehension only affected the productivity in a marginal way. Social Matching Effects and Group Productivity Illusions also lessen productivity. But it was the Blocking that they noticed really reduced the number of ideas that a group could contribute.

That's right; the number of ideas that can be generated is limited by the fact that only one person can talk at a time. What should this mean for you? If you are designing a brainstorming session, try to come up with a way for people to record their ideas while the discussion is going.

There is a pretty strong argument for working as a team. For one thing, it helps people focus. With all the distractions from different forms of information it is very difficult to take time and really engage in what you need to do. If you have a team, a time set aside, and a place to do it, then it's much easier to get into the mode of being creative. It's a way of using our social instincts to an advantage.

Another compelling reason is because in many cases the problems we are trying to solve are simply too difficult to solve well as an individual. It requires a multidisciplinary team simply to understand the problem space.

How a Team Can Help You

Many of the problems that hold us back with new ideas can be solved by working as a team instead of as an individual. For instance, let's go back to the problems broken out in the previous chapter:

- Staying focused
- Killing our ideas too quickly.
- Remembering our ideas
- Falling in love with our ideas
- Feature Hoarding

Working with one other person to brainstorm and write down the ideas can solve all of these problems. If you have one friend to talk about your ideas with, they can keep you from falling in love with your ideas or adding too many features. If you are too critical maybe they are too optimistic. You don't have to be perfectly balanced as long as there are the right personalities to balance out the group. What you need to form is an ideation group or what I call a think tank.

The best reason to form a think tank is because you need to find people of a similar mindset who will be able to give you criticism and to help you to continue thinking about your ideas. This sort of group comes with a price. The price is trust and control. Ideas are shared thoughts. To get the benefit of another person's evaluation of your idea, you must first share the idea with that person. But in doing so, you have now given it away and that idea may now be outside your control. What you should realize is that the people you tell your idea to are not your competition. You will never know that competition until you see your idea actually created by someone else. So if you do have an amazing idea, tell it to someone you trust immediately.

But wait, you might say, this creates a new problem: you cannot tell that idea to just anyone. Some people do not understand the joy of creating ideas. They simply do not feel it themselves and it isn't something they do. This doesn't mean they cannot learn this practice, but if they do not care then they probably are not going to participate or improve. You cannot make someone into an ideation partner; they have to choose to be one. This means that you need to find people and after you find them you need to put your trust in them.

Sounds like a long road, doesn't it? It really isn't. In six months you could have an idea group to bounce ideas around with. But it is up to you to start that process of finding them and helping them.

Idea Ownership

When talking about an idea, I sometimes fear that I will lose control of it. This fear isn't without justification. I'm sure everyone can rattle off a story or two of someone who talked about an idea and then lost control of it. My best story for that would be a professor I once worked for who invented a special sap probe for analyzing plants. Lets call him Dr. Plant. He invented this while working on his Ph.D. Somehow Dr. Plant's major professor's son ended up with the patent. It's pretty much unfair, and he did lose control of what he had invented. But I don't know if that is a failure on his part or if that is simply a failure of the character of the person who stole it. From that point onward, Dr. Plant would teach other people how to manufacture the probe on their own. The son did create a version that could be bought commercially. I think in the end the way to make this right would have been to give credit to the originator or to give him some share in the business.

So, yeah, there are stories of bad people who take what isn't theirs and get away with it. It's also easy to rationalize this sort of thing with "well the consumer won in the end" or "that patent expires in 20 years" or even "boys will be boys". All of these take the edge off the annoyance, but I think the real damage happens with how we want to adjust our behavior to deal with it.

Here is an alternate story that illustrates the opposite situation. A few years back my team and I decided to build a check-in app. It was called www.megosi.com. We put around 2000 man-hours into creating this app that lets you build a scavenger hunt to share. This was around the time that Foursquare, Gowalla, and everyone else was creating a check-in app. We got something together pretty fast, in the order of months. But, ultimately it didn't go anywhere. The big question is this: Why did Megosi fail? There are several reasons, but the most likely reason was we didn't get enough publicity behind it and we didn't know how to develop that business. I believe the difference between success and failure for Megosi was we needed to know "that person" with a rolodex or a book, or the most read blog, or something to help us drive people to our check-in app vs someone else's. There could have been hundreds of other reasons, but I'm pretty sure it wasn't because Foursquare was faster at shipping their app.

My point is that I needed more skills on my team. How quickly we got to market was not the issue. Keeping the idea to myself didn't change time-to-market for anyone else. I am sure there were hundreds of us that came up with the same idea but, it was the team that made it a success.

The lesson I have come away with is this: the more you share idea the stronger it will become. Also, the more you share, the more people you will attract to the idea. If it is a really good idea, a team will form around it. If two teams form around it, consider ways to bring them together.

I will be the first to admit that I have trouble opening up about my real ideas. I feel like I have a special reserve that I still hold in secret. But, the longer I hold them inside, the more I realize that I don't have the time or energy to do any of these by myself. At some point I will see my idea pop up on the Internet.

Who is on your team?

Personalities and how they add to your group

I do not like putting people into boxes. In truth we are all unique snowflakes of wants, needs, desires, flaws, and passions. Given five minutes we will shift around. As soon as you generalize any group of people, step in and get to know them, and you will notice that none of them are the same.

You can spend a whole lifetime just trying to get to know one person and only then find an aspect of them you never noticed. Just think of yourself. You can spend a lifetime just trying to figure out yourself and most likely, you never will understand yourself completely.

Regardless, it is very helpful to abstract some personality types. I won't say that everyone fits these archetypes, but they probably will act in one of these roles at some point. It is important to be aware of this because this will dictate the "vibe" of your think tank.

If you can control it you will most likely want a mix of personalities. But then again, controlling it may only stifle what could have happened.

The following are a list of personality archetypes I have encountered. You might fit into one or many of these. It might depend upon the weather.

Entrepreneur

These are the doers of the group. Usually applying some sort of driving force, usually articulate, sometimes connected, but searching for problems to solve if enough people are affected by the problem. They get frustrated if the ideas don't go anywhere and tend to shy away from ideas that don't have any tangible need to them. The biggest problem I have found with entrepreneurs is that they have a little trouble "playing" with ideas.

One really strong aspect is they tend to judge with their gut. If they "feel" like an idea is good then it usually means there is some reason why that idea is very good but, it will take a while to tease out the reason. They will also figure out how to take a rather bizarre idea and turn it into something other people want.

Evangelist

They love everything. If someone talks it is gold. They are the cheerleaders of the group and will keep everyone motivated and having a good time. They really enjoy the attention of the group and might sometimes take over the conversation or the whole group. But they are wonderful to have around because they keep the energy level high. They love to point out bigger and bigger opportunities and usually have a salesman's charisma, charming the group.

Scientist

Science trains people to be critical of ideas. It's built into the scientific method, and to the rest of us this could feel like they are just shooting down ideas. These people will be the best analysts of the group. They will methodically review all the assumptions that give an idea any strength. But if you can get an idea past them, it is probably pretty solid. They will be the best judges of the group.

Artist

The artists I know work very hard to leave their minds open to all possibilities. The ones that I have brainstormed with come up with all sorts of things. Their downside is a tendency to go off-topic and stay there. The upside, however, is that they get everyone else to think more and stretch their minds. You can always filter the ideas down later.

Hacker

They love to show how brilliant they are, and usually there is no denying that they are. In my experience, folks who have a hacker background love to push the social boundaries. The ideas they generate are wild, sometimes illegal, perhaps dangerous, but they will think so far out of the box that you aren't even sure where the box went.

Engineer

Engineers are like hackers, but they don't rebel as easily. They will have a lot of knowledge on some obscure subjects. The downside is some of the smartest engineers I know are also very very reserved. They will have some amazing ideas deep down inside and teasing those ideas out is sometimes the hardest thing to do. They don't usually like being the center of attention, but they are happy to help others by adding to their ideas.

Engineers often have intimate knowledge of something very specific and have studied a variety of topics in detail throughout their lives. So their ideas will be flavored with these experiences. I have also noticed that the rebel attitude shows up a lot. But this could be good because it gets the rest of the group thinking differently.

I'm sure there are many more types of personalities that can contribute. Each with their own title. I'm also sure that each of us have been more than one of these personalities in our lives. Ultimately you can use something like Myers-Briggs personality indicator to mix and match traits and form new personality buckets.

Mixing it up

There are many ways to generalize people. The point isn't to put people into boxes or over-analyze this. Instead, when you create your group, make sure you don't have too much of one kind of personality. Approach groups of people and organizations to try and get a good mix of different people from different spaces. A common problem is that these different groups tend to form cliques and isolate themselves from each other. Our strength is in our differences, however; you will see the effect immediately when a hacker is talking about an idea to overthrow the phone company and the entrepreneur realizes this is a very clever disruptive technology that might help solve a common problem. Or when the engineer finally starts talking and the evangelist runs with the idea giving the engineer the confidence to actually build it.

Sometimes you will look around a table of people from very different backgrounds and hear ideas mutating, changing, and growing, and realize that the only part of this situation you can control is who you can approach and get to show up. Everything else is due to the people in the group and you are at that moment just riding a wave of ideas.

Groups Build Stronger Ideas

Ideas start as connections in your mind between different subject matters. To improve these ideas other people need to review them, so you must share them. What stops us from sharing is the feeling that we are giving something up - as if, after the idea leaves us, we can no longer control its destiny. But to truly evaluate the idea, you must tell other people and trust that they will not take your idea. You must get past this feeling of loss.

Start building that trustable group with which you can talk about your ideas. It would be best to include several people who each have a different view on what you are doing. Talk to your engineering friend, your artist friend, and your business friend. Try talking to lots of people. After you have some faith that the idea isn't completely a bad idea, start talking to people you don't know as well. If you can find a way to talk to someone about your idea whom you trust - and who you trust to be honest with you - that is the best combination. The reason for this is simple: the more you share your idea with others, the stronger it will become, and the more confident you will become in its future prospects.

Raw ideas have to come from individuals, but to refine them you need to talk to many people. If you simply like talking about ideas, you may consider forming an 'idea group.' A group can push your thoughts on a subject. Depending on the type of people in the group you could end up learning more about a subject or just forming an idea that never would have come about before.

The next chapter focuses on how to build a group if you don't already have one. This group will form a sounding board of sorts, off of which you can bounce your ideas.

Chapter 3: DIY Think Tank

To explore ideation with groups I brought together several people who were interested in practicing brainstorming techniques and called it the Seattle Think Tank. The group was open to whoever wanted to come to the event. We have been meeting since 2009 trying different brainstorming exercises and ways to look at ideas.

In working with folks in Seattle about Ideation I have learned a lot about how to put a group together and what to do with them once they are together. This chapter is devoted to describing what was learned and how you could repeat what was done.

At some level you will want a group of people with whom to talk about ideas simply for feedback purposes. As that group gets bigger or otherwise goes through changes, the lessons learned in this chapter will help you to direct what is going on within that group. In the grander theme of this book you will need an idea team to provide a source of ideas for your incubator in general. These people may be able to meet more regularly and with more continuity between sessions. Use this chapter to design and focus your group to provide a source of ideas.

Building a Think Tank

To start putting together your think tank you really just have to start asking people to join you for idea brainstorming. I call such gatherings "idea sprints" and tend to have them in the evening. Start by picking a time and place and then getting 4 - 9 people to show up. Set aside two hours for the entire session. Obviously, you can change these parameters to meet your group's expectations, but that gives you a starting point.

If you get more than nine people, then try splitting it into two groups. The reason for this is because in larger groups some people tend to stop participating. It is a bit of a balance that you will have to work with to try to get input from everyone who is involved. At a certain point, however, the more introverted folks will step back and let the louder people run the whole show. This isn't really the best outcome if you're hoping to get lots of ideas out of the group.

As for how much time to set aside, I recommended two hours simply because people get tired working like this. It takes a bit of energy and emotion. So make sure that everyone has eaten something first and that there is some way to keep the group's blood sugar up. People tend to get crankier when they are hungry and that will also block the progress of your group. You could put a day into this sort of activity but, I think it might be too much for some folks. A couple of hours is just about as much extroverted energy as some people can muster.

What is the format of the meetings?

The entire purpose of creating your think tank is to promote face to face discussions of ideas. With that in mind you can and should experiment with the format and the activities your think tank promotes. The following is what we do. This should give you a basic idea of what you might consider doing as well.

Before the Sprint

It's important to get an idea of how many people are going to show up to your meeting. For that you simply have to ask people to commit. Pick a date and post a sign-up form. If not enough people sign up, then try a different date.

> ## Before the sprint checklist
>
> - Sign up form will be sent out 2 weeks in advance
> - 1 week out we will notify people they are on the list.
> - 3 days before a reminder will be sent out
> - At the session, name badges will be provided, people will be encouraged to include their name and a word to describe themselves

Do realize that organizing people is an art form in itself and outside the scope of this book. In my experience if you have a group of 100 people, 10 of them will sign up. Of that 10, half will actually show up. You will also, however, get three additional people randomly showing up. So from 100 people you should be able to get around eight to participate.

Give people at least two weeks to plan out their schedule and then remind them occasionally.

During the Sprint

The sprint itself consist mostly of the Mental Exercises. We try to fit in two per night. The first one always just helps people start talking and for the group to begin to think together. The second one is where people really get to let loose and start brainstorming as a team.

For the most part these mental exercises are somewhat like party games with brainstorming. I have listed several mental exercises later in this chapter.

During the sprint checklist

- Mental Exercise: 45 minutes
- Break : 10 minutes to record ideas
- Mental Exercise: 45 minutes
- Record ideas and metrics: 10 minutes
- Cool down period; discuss, debate, and think.

After the Sprint

Make sure you have a plan to hang out with your group after the sprint. We have found that people need to let off some steam and talk about ideas and what came out of the sprint. This is also where a lot of people have a chance to find out who they were talking to and to talk about other random ideas that were not brought up during the sprint.

> ## After the sprint checklist
>
> ✓ Tell your group how it went
>
> ✓ Send out a list of the ideas from that night
>
> ✓ Record your observations and notes to improve

Documenting

While the idea sprint is in progress, make sure you are collecting the ideas somewhere. Write them down somewhere, or have people fill out cards periodically with the high-point ideas that they've come up with. You will want to collect these and later send them back out to your group. The reason for this is that a good portion of the best ideas will come up later as 'residual ideas' where someone has thought about a discussion from the night before and realizes a solution that is much better than what was said by anyone previously.

By providing the list of ideas in a documented format you will allow everyone to remember what was previously discussed so they can add to this.

Tip 1: Create a common idea repository

In working on finding a way to document these ideas we

ended up building a system that allows us to store and add to ideas later. We called it trydea and it is an open-source project that anyone can setup and use to create their own repository online for their group. Feel free to use our system.

If Trydea doesn't work for you all you really need is a common place to store everyones idea. For instance, a wiki, google doc, or a even just a file cabinet.

What Mental Exercises should you do?

This is really the core of the experience. You can get a bunch of people together to brainstorm and then just have the whole thing fall apart. What you really need is an activity for everyone to do. The next section is devoted to just this. We spent a considerable amount of time trying out different activities to see what works and what doesn't.

I would highly recommend that you try to do something that gets everyone talking for the first exercise. Most people need to warm up and to become more vocal and less introverted. Then really try to go for volume on the second exercise. The obvious reason for this is that people usually are somewhat shy. So make sure everyone gets a chance to talk in the first round to get any self-consciousness out of the way.

One other thing to point out is that these activities themselves are ones that have worked for us, but you can mix and match parts to design your own activities. So think of the different parts as components that you can mix and match. Some parts of the activities will be better at accomplishing a task than others. For instance, having one person pitch and then be questioned is great for digging into one idea deeply. While having activities like Idea Handoff are better for getting large volumes of ideas. It really depends on the goals of your Idea Sprint. Is it to get people thinking, to think through a particular idea or theme, or perhaps to generate lots of ideas?

I should also note that there are other books that have done a fantastic job of talking about the other components of this brainstorming activity. Look for the book *Game Storming* by Dave Grey. I discovered his book years after I started doing this, but he provides lots of good component activities that you can use to create new exercises to do with your Think Tank.

> ### Tip 2: Bring an Oven Timer
> The following exercises are to get folks talking. Its more important to get everyone talking than to fully think through the idea. Use an oven timer (or stopwatch, or smartphone app, or whatever) to keep things moving.

Warm-up exercises

Mental Exercise 1: Worst Idea. Have everyone fix it.

The purpose of this activity is to help people get past the idea of having bad ideas. It also helps to form the team because they are all trying to help to improve the idea.

Step 1: 4 minutes of silence

Have everyone write down two ideas that are awful. Maybe their own ideas, maybe ideas they spontaneously came up with. Maybe ideas heard from another source.

Step 2: Put it in a box

Collect all the bad ideas together and then pick a person to start with.

Step 3: Take turns to randomly draw and improve the idea (3 minutes)

Have the first person pull an idea from the box at random. He or she then reads the idea, and the group attempts to brainstorm ways to improve it.

Step 4: Pass the box on

The next person to the left gets either to draw a new idea or to try improving the previous idea further.

Step 5: Continue for 45 minutes

Keep going around the circle drawing ideas and improving upon them until you have either done this for 45 minutes or run out of ideas.

Step 6: Record ideas

Give everyone a chance to write down the ideas they linked and to collect those into a separate pile.

Mental Exercise 2: Idea Cluster

The purpose of this exercise is to create a high volume of interesting ideas. It also should get us thinking creatively and breaking away from what we did during the day.

Step 1: Get a list of topics

Everyone gets three minutes to talk about the subjects they are following. What are they? Why are they interested? These are written on the board.

Step 2: Idea Race (5 minutes)

We break into teams of two, then get five minutes to come up with as many ideas related to these topics as possible. Write these on post-it notes. They don't have to be based on the topics, but use the topics as inspiration.

Step 3: Put all the post-its on the board

Put all the post-its on the board. Remove duplicates and as a team start grouping them together to form a giant map of ideas. Ideas should form into clusters.

Step 4: Save the good ones!

We will write down the best of these ideas and we should take a picture of what formed on the board.

Mental Exercise 3: Spontaneous Theme + Pitch

Use this exercise to help people settle on a theme, solve a problem, and then pitch. In a way this is the first step toward all business ventures and is good practice.

First brainstorm some themes

Step 1: Get suggestions

Go around the group and asked everyone to suggest one or two themes. Have someone write these on the whiteboard.

Step 2: Vote on the themes

Everyone has two votes and makes a mark next to the themes they liked best. Each person goes up to the board and puts two marks next to two different themes.

Step 3: Reduce to 5

Erase all but the five most popular themes. Now you have some subjects to focus on.

Step 4: Generate 'idea fodder' (3 minutes)

Have everyone take three notecards and write down three nouns related to the themes left on the board. The reason you do this is to provide 'idea fodder' without forcing people to work in a broad theme. It is much easier to come up with an idea such as "using offshore wind energy to help homeless people" instead of "come up with something in ecology".

Step 5: Collect the idea fodder together

Make a deck out of all the cards and shuffle them.

Now pitch

Step 6: Pull two cards and come up with an idea to sell (3 minutes)

Pick someone to start; he or she gets the deck of cards. Have this person draw two cards and then try to sell an idea he or she comes up with. If someone gets stuck, the group can help him before the timer runs out.

Step 7: Pass the deck to the next person.

Pass the deck to the person on the first person's left. Now this person pulls two cards and repeats the process.

> #### Tip 3: Bad ideas are good conversation.
> The idea doesn't have to be good. In fact it might be worth saying, "come up with your worst idea using those words." This helps participants to relax and stop trying to provide the correct idea.

Mental Exercise 4: Idea Hand-off

This is a little like the telephone game meets ideation. It is great to generate lots of ideas and to get people talking. This exercise is great because it gets confusing and ideas all start mingling after a while. It helps people separate themselves from the ideas.

Step 1: Configure the team

Get the group into a relatively circular formation with an even number of people. Everyone in the ring needs a conversation partner. So make sure everyone knows if he is suppose to be talking to the person to his left or right.

Step 2: Get your 'seed ideas' (1 minute)

Give everyone a moment to think of an idea. It doesn't have to be good.

Step 3: Explain ideas (4 minutes)

You tell your partner your idea and he tells you his.

Step 4: Switch partners

When the timer beeps you need to stop talking to your current partner and then turn either to your right or left and find your new conversation partner.

Step 5: Explain the idea you just heard to your new partner (4 minutes)

Now explain the idea you just heard from your first partner to your new partner. This 'hands off' the idea to the new person. They also will tell you an idea.

Step 6: Switch and explain again (4 minutes)

Now repeat the process from Step 5. Thus you are becoming a vehicle for the idea itself. You will notice that if the idea is good then it is easy to explain. If it doesn't make any sense you will figure out a better way to explain it.

> Tip 4: Fixing bad ideas.
> Tell your participants "If If you don't like the idea, change it until you do." This helps to not just judge, but to contribute based on a judgement.

Step 7: Finishing

You can do this until the ideas have had a chance to go around the table. Repeat it at many times as there are people. You can stop at any point. To finish the exercise have each person speak about one idea he or she ended up with. This is mostly so people can see how their idea has changed.

Exercises for Quality

Mental Exercise 5: Pitch and Discuss

This is a chance to get feedback on an idea. It requires that people come to the event with an idea in mind. You can also start the idea sprint by telling people that you are looking for volunteers who would be interested in receiving feedback about an idea.

It is very helpful for the person to hear the reasoning of the reviewer and why he feels the way he does. The pitch then becomes a way to generate discussion around the idea.

Step 1: Presenter pitches (3 minutes)

Have the presenter stand up and explain his or her idea. The presenter receives three minutes in which to do so.

Step 2: Group discuss (10 minutes)

As a group we get to talk about it. Talk about the pros and cons of the idea.

Step 3: Create a Fun Money Grid and rate it

On a piece of paper or a whiteboard draw two cardinal axes and label them as follows:

Step 4: Let each reviewer explain how he feels about his mark.

After someone has pitched an idea, have each person go up to the board and make a mark where he or she thinks the idea rates in terms of how much fun it will be to build and how much it will be worth.

Note: This technique is explained in more detail in Chapter 4.

Exercise 6: Team Pitch

To do this exercise you need three decks of note cards of different colors. You will have your team create 'aspects' on each card, and then each person will work to come up with ideas based on these aspects.

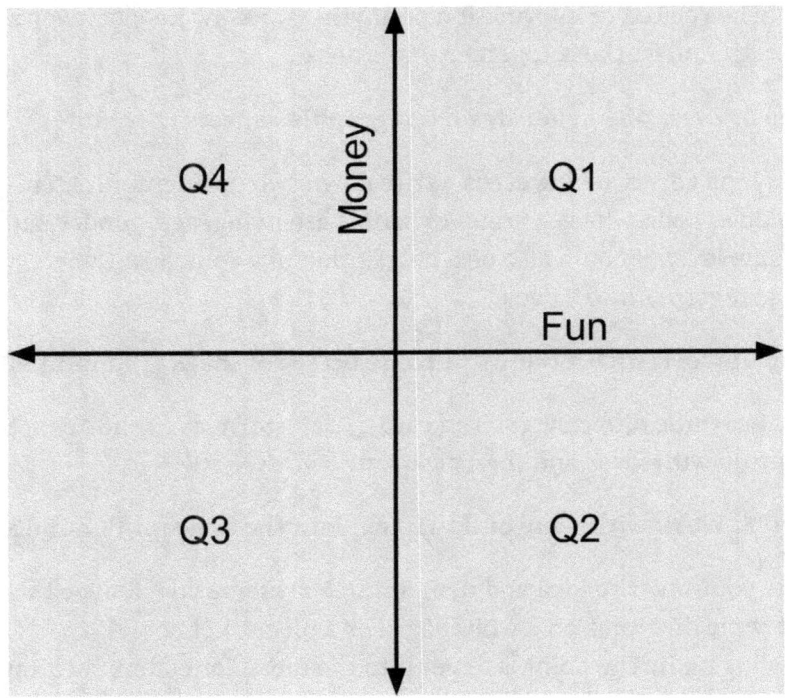

I suggest the following:

- Red cards have a technology written on them
- Green cards have a problem written on them
- Blue cards have a demographic or audience written on them

Step 1: Everyone generates problem aspects (2 minutes)

Everyone gets two green cards. Each person writes down two problems he or she is thinking about. These could be worldly problems or just things that person has noticed. Collect these together into a deck.

Step 2: Everyone generates technology aspects (2 minutes)

Everyone gets two red cards. Write down two technologies. They could be related to information or anything, really. Just an invention of sorts. Collect these together into a deck.

Step 3: Everyone generates demographic aspects (2 minutes)

Everyone gets two blue cards. Write down two demographics. This should explain where a group of people are living, age, gender, and income level. It could also be a description of a company. Collect these together into a deck.

Step 4: Work with a buddy to come up set of ideas (10 minutes)

You get three different colored cards. Brainstorm as a mini-team to come up with ideas and then pick your favorite.

Step 5: Work with your buddy to explain the concept (5 minutes)

Take your favorite idea and turn it into a presentation. Maybe this is just some diagrams on a whiteboard or a piece of paper with a drawing on it. The point is to get into the mode for communicating your idea.

Step 6: Make Presentations (90 seconds each)

Each team will then tell the problem, technology, and demographic that they are working with and their idea. Try to sell people on this.

Step 7: Cross examine (3 minutes)

Let everyone ask questions of the idea. Let the presenters defend it.

Brainstorming on a subject

Notice that all of the exercises listed did not require a particular theme. Those exercises are fairly general-purpose and can be used to just get people thinking. At various times, however, you might want to have people focus on something in particular for an entire evening. In this way, it becomes less about ideation techniques and instead about applying the group to a problem.

This is a different kind of meeting and should be explained this way: The problem you will run into is settling on the theme you want to use. If you pick a theme no one is interested in, then too few people will come. If you list a set of meetings and apply a theme to each one then people will only show up for ones they are interested in. For this to work you really need your Think Tank to collectively want to focus on a subject.

So then the question becomes, "What theme would be interesting?". I would ask that you phrase this in the form of a question instead of a statement. For instance, it is much easier to focus on "How can we use wind power effectively?" than just saying "The theme is windpower."

Tip 5: Use questions to drive conversation.
Questions get people thinking faster than telling them to randomly generate something with a subject.

The final problem that is tricky is that if people are given a theme and they know nothing on that topic, then what? This is where you need a deeper commitment from your Think Tank. They can't just show up to the idea night. Now they need to have homework. Here is the crux of the problem. People are generally overworked already and if they are showing up to a social event that requires homework they tend to not do this.

There are a couple of things that work here. You can ask people to show up with three ideas related to the theme already. That means they are thinking about it. You can also set aside a little time before the event so that folks can do some quick research and come up with ideas on the spot. Finally you can repeat the theme more than once. This helps to get people to research between events and keep the conversation going.

If you are really focused on a particular theme you might limit your Think Tank to only ideas in this realm. For instance, nothing says you cannot create the Detroit Environmental Think Tank.

Growing your Think Tank

After conducting an "idea sprint" with a couple of friends you may want to start to grow the group and make it more of a regular event.

Start by naming your group. Choose a name that is available online and then buy it. You don't need a fancy website, but reserve it because it is helpful to have a web address to point people to. Since it will be important to meet physically somewhere to talk together, it might make sense to use the name of your city in it, or a local landmark. Something to state that your think tank happens around here. This is exactly the reasoning behind our group, the Seattle Think Tank.

Now you need a way to communicate with anyone who wishes to be part of your group. For this I highly recommend an email mailing list at minimum. These are so easy to set up on Google or Yahoo! that there really is no reason not to. Facebook, LinkedIn, Meet-up, I think there must be hundreds of online utilities for allowing communities to form. It really makes sense to use the format that your members will respond to the best. This may even be just a bulletin board in the lobby of your church or a calling tree. It really depends on your group and the way they feel most comfortable communicating.

One really helpful part about Google Groups is that they also have a calendar and that is the next piece you will need. It is much easier for people to know what to do if they know when it is happening. It will take a while to work out the best times to meet. No one's schedule ever matches up and there is always overlap. But, just remember as long as one person shows up to talk about ideas then it was a success.

Finally the last piece you need is a place to meet. If you don't have access to a house, try reserving a room at the library, your church, or a school classroom. It just needs to be a safe place with few distractions, access to a restroom and somewhere easy to find. Try thinking outside the box. Contact startups in the area and ask if you can use their space. Maybe you can use a business in its off-hours.

Finding people

Finding people could be as simple as putting up a sign in a lobby with your mailing list name on it. It needs to have an explanation of what you are doing, what to expect, when to meet and where. I have been explaining our think tank as a self-help group for inventors and entrepreneurs. When we get together we play what amounts to a party game involving brainstorming ideas. This is a pretty simple message to explain and usually it's enough for them to try it once.

The real trick at this point is figuring out where the right people for this would be looking. Sure, putting a sign on a street corner might work, but it is less likely. What I always want is to have a mix of personalities. So try not to get only the same type of people in the room together. Maybe some are entrepreneurs and others are artists.

Think Tank Roles

In running many ideation meetings with a think tank, I have found that certain roles need to be filled. If no one takes on these roles and you don't delegate them, then you will be the one who ends up filling all of them.

Coach

This person explains the rules, brings the equipment and helps keep everyone organized. He or she should also provide a small writeup after every event to tell the rest of the group how things went and how to improve them.

Recorder

This person is responsible for collecting the ideas that the group wants to hold onto from the Idea Sprint. He or she then has some way to get these ideas back to the Curator for the whole group.

Curator

This person is responsible for gathering the ideas and any

other information generated by the group. He or she may not enter all of the information themselves, but this person is responsible for defining how this information is stored and where. The Curator also tries to keep things organized so that other people can find what they are looking for.

Promoter

This person's responsibility is to find and involving new members. He or she is tasked with writing about what the think tank does and reaching out to contact new individuals.

Scheduler

This person handles sending out email, scheduling events, and making sure the space is available.

Concluding

If you want your ideas to improve you need to talk to someone. If you want different kinds of feedback then you need to talk to more than one person. If you want to go even further and have this group of people contribute you need a team that meets regularly. This is what I call a *Think Tank*. We have now covered what you need to do to create a Think Tank and to grow it.

Your Think Tank is a source of ideas and inspiration for business and hobbies. It also provides a foundation for networking within the group. What you will notice is that this lets people not just have fun with ideas, but also get to know each other around a common interest. Thus it becomes an important source of both ideas and teams.

For more ideas to generate ideas I would highly recommend the book *"Gamestorming"* by Dave Gray. It will help you build up more activities to do with your Think Tank.

Chapter 4: Judging Ideas

After running several idea sprints you will start to accumulate ideas. You should put these somewhere. Write them down on something so your group can find them again. But what do you do with them? How do you pare the list down to something of value? How do people grow the idea into something larger?

At the heart of it you should allow your group to look through the list of ideas and add comments to them. They should be able to find and talk about the ideas that really catch their imaginations. The ideas that they really like might just help to ignite action. But the list could get large. It will help to sort and filter the ideas.

The way you choose to do this is going to come down to your group and what you are looking for. Maybe you are looking for a great project, or the way to best use your time, or maybe you want to start a business and need the best idea possible to get going with it.

The following are a list of suggested ways to pare down the ideas and to group them. Any of these activities might help you to find what you are looking for. I don't think that there is a "proven" way to actually find the "best" idea. What these methods will do is to start you on a journey to figure out what it is you are looking for in an idea and to find the one most successful for you.

The Idea Funnel

In general the process is to take a large number of ideas and to boil it down to the best idea. The crux here is "what do we mean by 'best?'". In this case it isn't just the most valuable or the most fun idea, but also the idea that is best aligned with you and your team. The idea should have a personal connection to you and your team. There will be many difficult moments after you decide to implement an idea, and without this connection you and your team could very well lose focus.

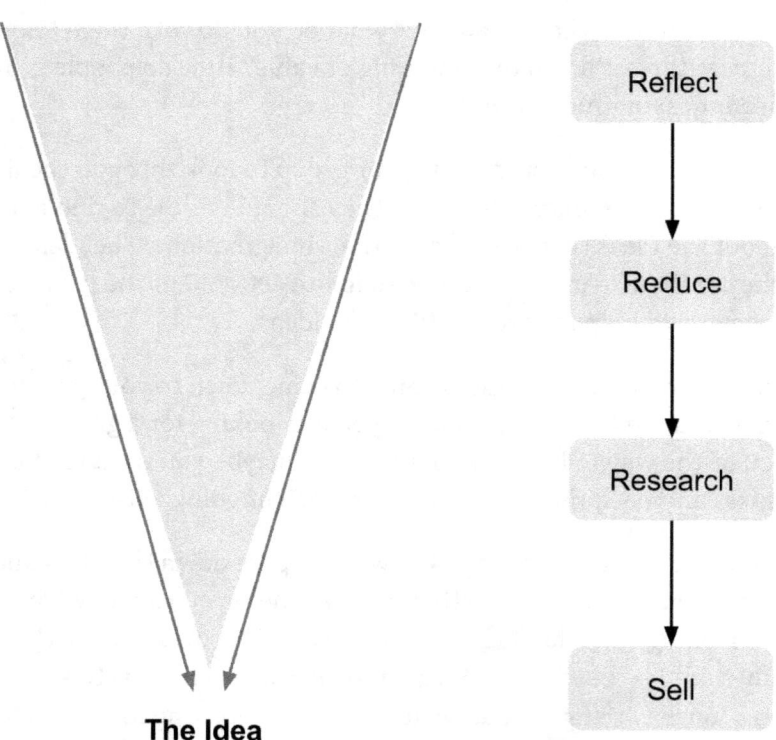

This process is designed to take a large list of ideas and reduce it down to the best ones. The rest of this chapter introduces activities that will help you to get through this process. However, this is by no means an exhaustive list. These activities were found either by interviewing people or by testing them within our ideation community. I expect there are many other great techniques and activities that could help, and I encourage you to invent your own. The general structure, however, will break down to the following process: Reflect, Triage, Research, and Sell.

Step 1: Reflect

Before you can decide on the best idea for you, you need to figure out what you are looking for. Start by answering this question:

Do you want to use this idea to make money?

If you start off building a "cool" idea that you are excited about, but in the back of your mind you are hoping that you will just get lucky and invent something valuable, then you will burn yourself out. If you are going to build a business, then start off with that as your focus. If you want to lose yourselves as an explorer of technology, then go that route. Just don't straddle this line.

The reason I say this is that business ideas require you to think about how other people will use what you are making. You will be judged by your customers and if you don't start from the get-go thinking about them, then you are depending entirely on luck. Project ideas depend on your passion and the passion of the other contributors. Those other contributors might not care what other people think and it will just confuse the group. Half of you are building something with the hope to sell it, and the other half are just enjoying the passion of building.

Reflect Technique 1: Finding a Feeling

How you "feel" about an idea may be the most important factor when shopping for an idea. Not just whether you like it, but the actual feeling that you want the idea itself to express. The reason is simple: If you don't feel passion for an idea, you will not be able to sell it to other people, your founders, or even to yourself. If you can't sell it, you will not be able to convince anyone to help you with it, help fund it, or to buy it. Even if the idea is just for you, knowing how you want to feel about the idea will help you select the best one.

What this process is for is to help you build up your intuition. If you are looking for an idea to run with and you suspect that you'll only get one chance at it, it makes sense to find an idea that you feel the strongest about. This is a very counterintuitive approach to our logical minds, which prefer to label and quantify items.

Instead this technique helps you form a vision for where you want to be. The thought here is that if you run into hard times, as long as you still have this vision in your heart then you'll know what to do next. It becomes your compass for where you want to go next.

Vision Process

What you are hunting for is a memory, a deed from your past that you were proud of or that made you feel "right". This could be anything from racing down a hill on a snowboard to talking with your grandmother. In any case, every memory you have is associated with a feeling. And we are hunting for a feeling that defines how you want to feel about the idea you are about to commit yourself to.

Step 1: Find a place to focus.

Find a time when you don't have any distractions. I prefer the early morning or the late evening. Put on headphones, drive, run, do what you need to do to get yourself into a relaxed state and essentially meditate.

Step 2: Review your life.

Now start thinking of memories that you have had that made you feel excited about what you were doing. Maybe it was when you were racing down a hill on a bike, or maybe when you had completed a thesis. It could be when you made your first dollar, or when you were just helping out a friend. As you go back in time through your mind, re-live some of these experiences and remember how you felt.

Step 3: Find the memory.

At some point you will find a memory that represents excitement to you. That is now your guiding memory and it helps you find that emotion that you will be looking for as you move forward. Maybe write it down somewhere special, or email it to yourself. Or, simply make note of it in your mind. It is a special memory to you and when you recall it, it makes you feel something.

Step 4: Grow the memory.

From time to time, come back to the memory. Add details to it, give it more definition. The memory will continue to get more detailed as it refines the feeling that you want your ideas to represent to you.

Step 5: Using the guiding memory.

As you look for ideas, founders, and direction, keep pulling that memory up. If you are faced with a decision or need to make a choice, look at your choices and determine which one makes you feel closest to your "guiding memory". This emotion becomes a guiding compass or muse to help you make decisions.

Just a note: This is an intensely personal tool. By no means do you need to share it.

I want to thank Joe Justice who founded Wikispeed for this insight. He told me how he has used this leadership tool when working on his crowdsourced car company.

Reflect Technique 2: Find your Founders

Founders are the people who initiated the idea. There may be many other followers later, but the founders were there before the idea happened and end up becoming the driving influence if the idea is implemented successfully.

Why?

If you will have only one founder, then you can do all of this in isolation. If you plan on having two founders, however, you will need to work through these exercises together or you both might be thinking differently. If you fail to get the founders' mutual buy-in from the beginning, then they are not truly founders and will most likely move on to other projects later.

Here is a handy trick for figuring out where you are strong and where you need help.

Step 1. List all the functions for your enterprise. These might be things like

- Project Management
- Accounting
- Marketing
- Sales
- System Administration

Step 2. Now put that into a spreadsheet with this list as the left column

Step 3. Across the top make two columns

Have Skills: *You already know how to do this*

Want Skills: *You would like to learn how to do this*

Step 4. Now fill in the grid with the numbers 0 to 10, where 10 represents the best score.

Step 5. Next, make one more column and subtract the have from the want to get a change score.

Step 6. Finally, make one more column and add the scores together. This gives you a strength score.

It should end up looking something like this.

Skills	Have Skills	Want Skills	Change Score	Strength Score
Accounting	8	3	-5	11
Marketing	6	6	0	12
Sales	2	4	2	6
Project Management	8	10	2	18

What you are looking at is a profile of the strengths and deficiencies in yourself. It really breaks down into four things:

	Strength Score > 10	Strength Score < 10
Change Score > 0	If you have skills and an interest in learning more, then, perfect! You should be in that role.	If you don't have skill but you have an interest, this also is good; you should take on this role unless someone else knows more than you.
Change Score < 0	You obviously can do this job, but you need a plan to hand it off to someone with more interest.	This is a role that you need to pay someone to do or to find a co-founder who can fill this hole.

As you go looking for a co-founder, have that person do this same exercise and then compare the results to see where you collectively need to find more help.

This is a very important part of finding a co-founder. If you both have all the same skills then it doesn't make much sense to be working together. It also will allow you to figure out early who gets to take on which role instead of both of you thinking you get to do what you consider the fun part.

One thing to note about this exercise is that it can be used with a group of people to find holes within a team. Simply tally all the scores from all the people and preform the same analysis.

Step 2: Reduce

Now that you have your founding team, objective, and a guiding passion, get all the founders together and open up your big pile of ideas. Go through these ideas, and by the end you should have just a few.

Reduction Technique 1: The Money/Fun Grid
A method for rapidly triaging ideas

Since your group has many different personalities with many different objectives it makes the most sense to divide the list up by what people are hunting for. Here is a suggestion, which we call the *money/fun grid*. This was the simplest possible way to get a crowd's response to an idea to see if they would be interested in pursuing it further.

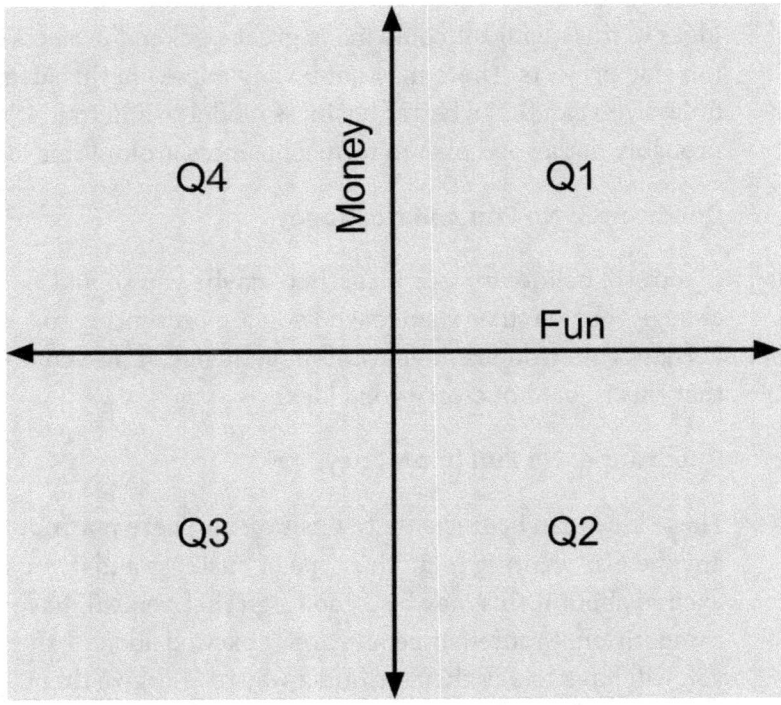

In the simplest terms, the vertical axis represents how much money this idea is worth, and the horizontal axis is how much fun it would be to make. After someone has heard an idea, ask him or her to place a dot on the grid. Placement near the center point means that person feels neutral. Notice that the grid axes have no numerical markers because this isn't a quantitative tool. What you want is to know what people instinctively feel toward the idea. Is it a good idea? Will it make money? Would it be fun to work on?

The quadrants become sets of ideas with the following properties.

Quadrant 1: Fun and Money

Clearly any idea that ends up in this area is something worth thinking about more.

Quadrant 2: Fun but No Money

Ideas in this quadrant could make great weekend projects or fun side projects. There may not be any money in this idea, so unless you can find a better business model to add to it, it's probably not a good plan to form a business around this idea.

Quadrant 3: No Fun and No Money

If you still believe in your idea, then maybe you should change your pitch or change who you are presenting to. Perhaps this group isn't your target audience. It also could be that this is just not a very good idea.

Quadrant 4: No Fun but Money

These ideas can be turned into businesses. There may not be anyone else wanting to do this type of business and if you are excited about it this may be a good sign that you will have less competition. Granted, if people aren't excited about it then you will have to pay them or find a way to energize them.

Any time you need to measure the gut reactions of a crowd to an idea this is an easy way to survey them. You can pretty much tell right from the beginning what sort of idea you are dealing with and what sort of project it could become. This is intended to drive conversation within the group, but you should consider having your team figure this out by themselves first. Then make the results visible. For instance consider a wall where people could mark on it after a everyone has had a chance to sort this out for themselves. This way the grid becomes a source of conversation that will help build crowd-consensus around a set of ideas. When you look at the results this is an easy way to intuitively judge what isn't going to work. You end up with 4 quadrants,

Reduction Technique 2: Fill in the blank business plans

An idea is a solution. And each solution solves a problem. But, when it comes to the impact of an idea it is very important to figure out who it solves the problem for and how many of these people there are. If you are going to build this idea as a business, then you need to have a rough idea of how much each of these people would be willing to pay. Finally, you need to have a plan for how you will create this idea. In this lies the rough format for a business plan.

To really sift through several ideas you probably don't want to write a business plan for each one. But, it is still important to think through where each idea fits into this puzzle. This exercise helps you by taking a larger set of ideas and figuring out a one-line business plan for each. Once you get used to thinking this way it becomes easier to compare two ideas against each other.

Step 1: Get your list of ideas together and gather your co-founders.

Step 2: Write all of the ideas you wish to analyze into some sort of document. You could use a whiteboard or anything that makes it easier to work together as a group.

Step 3: For each idea, apply this "Mad Libs" sentence format.

[name] is a [deliverable] that uses [technology] to solve [problem] for this [demographic].

Step 4: Now open up a spreadsheet and create five columns in it:

Name	Deliverable	Technology	Problem	Demographic

Write all of the information from each idea into the spreadsheet.

Step 5: The power here is in the ability to sort these ideas now. If you are going for impact, you might want to focus on the demographic. If your team wanted to build something in particular, or they have skills that match the technology, maybe those are the ideas you should focus on.

Granted, these will be actual sentences, so sorting might not work in your case. But, given 50 ideas, you will have patterns between ideas and they will collect together.

Step 6: Now eliminate ideas. When you look at ideas in this context it becomes much easier to compare them back and forth. You could go even further and add metrics such as the size of the population it will affect, how much you could make in sales, or how long it will take to build. But the point really is to look at these ideas, side by side, in an objective fashion.

What this exercise is designed to do is to to get a group of people together to discuss and to determine even further what they hope to accomplish. And even if you are a lone individual, it makes it much easier to assign values to attributes when comparing a large number of items.

Step 3: Research

By this step you should have a few ideas that fit your team. Now you need to reduce this further, and to do that, it's time to research.

Research Technique 1: Wave of Opportunity

From my experience with startups and ideas there is a wave that happens when a new market forms. If you were to look at the number of competitors over time the process would look like the following.

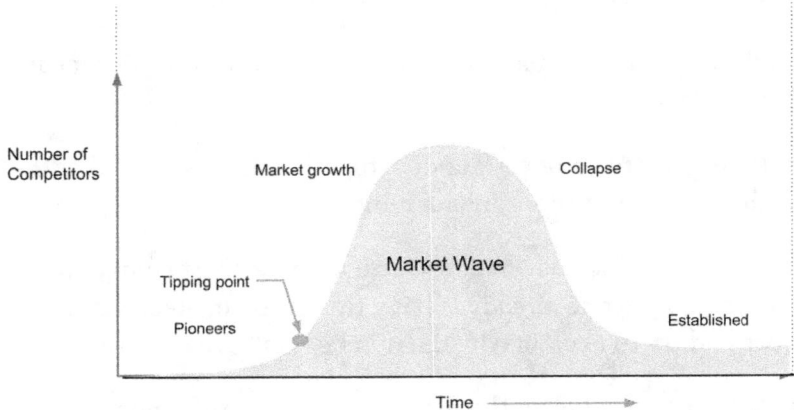

Essentially, as consumers learn of a new product or service it gets accepted into our culture. As that happens the market goes through different stages.

- Pioneers : Passionate groups struggle to solve problems.

- Tipping point: Someone is successful

- Market grows: Lots of fast followers jump on board pursuing the same idea.

- Collapse: The field narrows as all of the consumers decide on their favorite and reject the rest. The different competitors either fail or acquire each other

- Established market: Eventually you only have a small set of established competitors that continue to absorb each other.

With any idea, it's good to discover who may already be out there doing this before you start building it. Even more importantly, try to guess where this idea fits in this wave. Is the idea so new and novel that you would be a pioneer breaking new ground? Is this idea so overdone that there are already twenty startups trying this. As with surfing, you want to be in front of this wave. The real trick is figuring out how big the wave should be and how long it will last.

The following is a systematic way of figuring out where your ideas fit in this window.

Step 1: Get your team of co-founders together and list out all of the ideas that you are considering pursuing.

Step 2: As a group spend 30 minutes on each idea, list competitors and search for anyone already solving this problem. Record this number and try to explain why the number isn't greater or smaller.

Step 3: After reviewing all the ideas. Have every co-founder go down the list and tackle the question "where is the market wave for this idea?"

The point of this exercise isn't to discourage you. It's very important to note that even if there is a competitor, that doesn't mean that you shouldn't try your own hand at the problem. Sometimes it feels like a complete buzzkill to see that someone is already in that space. If this does destroy all of your momentum, perhaps you should look for an idea that is all about pioneering something absolutely unique. However, you should also think like an investor, because you are about to invest your time into a project. An item of importance to an investor is whether a market exists for an idea. If there are competitors, especially thriving ones, then that suggests it's an idea worth pursuing.

Research Technique 2: Five Sorted Criteria

To reduce your list of potential ideas it helps to define what you are looking for in an idea. It isn't enough to simply say, "Is this idea good?". After all, what is a "good" idea to you and your co-founders? At this point it is worth starting to move away from a gut reaction and to actually define what you are looking for in an idea.

One very likely set of criteria is the following. But, you don't need to limit yourselves to these:

- Cost : How much will it cost to build and operate for the first few months?

- Time : How much time will it take to create and operate?

- Quality : What level of quality is acceptable for your potential customer?

- Achievability : What are the chances that this idea is even possible?

- Ultimate Goal : Would the best future for this business be; going public, being acquired, cash cow?

The point is to start by thinking about what you are actually looking for when you look at a set of ideas. It is a good conversation for yourself and it is an even better conversation if you have co-founders.

Step 1: If you have co-founders, get them together in a room with a whiteboard.

Step 2: Get a stack of post-it notes and start writing down what is important to you, what you are looking for in a project/idea/start-up. As you come up with these criteria, stick them onto the whiteboard. Do this for 10 minutes or until you find yourself running out of steam.

Step 3: Start sorting the criteria; the higher up the board the more important it is to you.

Step 4: Now go down the list of criteria and compare them against one another. For example, is "Cost" more important to you than "Time?" If you compare them back and forth this way, after a while you'll have a prioritized list of all the criteria upon which you will judge the ideas.

Step 5: Now create a grid with the ideas you are judging on the right and the five criteria across the top. Fill in the area in the middle with a number that represents how well the idea satisfies the criteria. I would suggest you use 0 as "Worst" and 10 as "Best".

Step 6: Now you should tally up the score for the ideas. The ones that did well will end up with a much higher score, the others can be eliminated.

It might be helpful to do this last part with a spreadsheet. Calculating and sorting become much simpler. The downside is that if you are coming up with these numbers as a team, it might be a bit more difficult to get everyone's input if they must stand around a computer.

Step 4: Sell

By this point you should have a small set of well-thought-out ideas. Try these exercises to find out which you can sell. If you can get other people interested, you have a winner.

Sell Technique 1: Pitch Everything

If you enjoy talking to people then this approach might be a powerful technique for you to select one idea from a small set of ideas. For instance, let's say you have five ideas that you feel strongly about.

Step 1: For each idea figure out an elevator pitch. This means you need to come up with a one-sentence explanation for each idea.

Step 2: Now add a story to each idea to help others relate to it. Explain the problem it solves, who would use it, and how. This is your pitch.

Step 3: For the next 5 days, make each of these ideas the idea of the day. Pick one idea and pitch it to everyone; your neighbor, your roommate, random people at the bus stop. What reaction did they give you?

By the end of the week you should have a pretty good feel for how people think about those ideas. Is it having a positive response? Who is having a positive response? This is going to give you honest, genuine feedback because strangers don't have anything to hide. Just to note, don't talk to people who sugar-coat. Friends' evaluations aren't very good because they like you already. Make sure you get in front of people who will give you critical feedback.

Sell Technique 2: Market Your Ideas

Given a handful of ideas, one way to select the best is to simply try to sell it. With so many great ways to advertise online this can be pretty simple.

Step 1: Start with a landing page. You should create a one-page website where the only thing someone can do is sign up. This sign up could be through a form, a survey, Twitter; it doesn't really matter. You just need a way to measure interest. If they click on something, then they are interested. You should also go as far as to integrate an analytics package. Google is great here as well. Now you know how many people have come to your landing page, and how many actually did something.

Step 2: That landing page is now your goal in your marketing campaign. What you are going to try and do is to create a set of ads and figure out how much you need to pay people to click on them. At the time of writing this book, AdWords and Facebook ads are very simple ways to accomplish this. Both websites are self-explanatory as far as how this process works. When creating your campaign you get to see the rough cost that other people are bidding for on certain keywords. This can even give you some clues as to who else is out there and how large this market really is.

Step 3: Budget a little cash for your campaign and start it up. After a few days you can see pretty quickly how much interest people have in your idea as they work through the sales funnel. You can even play with different pricing to see if you can dial in what someone would actually pay for your idea.

The end result of this exercise is that you should have a much better feel of which idea you should be pursuing. What's also great is that you've already thought about what you might do to sell it. Crafting that message will be very difficult, but it helps to define what the product will be.

Sell Technique 3: Invest in Your Idea

When it comes down to it, the biggest test of an idea is if anyone would really invest in it. This might mean time, and this might mean money. But if someone is really willing to put resources into an idea then it may be a good one to build.

Your co-founders have already expressed that they want to work with you. But, are you all willing to pool your own money for resources?

One way to approach this is to make a small (10-page or so) slide show for each idea, called a *pitch deck*. Go through your presentation a couple of times and then actually pitch your idea to each other and then later to other people. Ask them if they are willing to invest and sign them up. What you are really looking for is if they are willing to say they will commit some cash to the idea - you're not necessarily asking them how much at this point.

This process won't just help you narrow down the last few ideas, it will tell you if any of these ideas are good enough to get people to believe in them. Additionally, you get to work on how you will present the idea to other people.

One thing to note is that you may never actually take them up on the investment. When you add an investor you need to realize that you are entering into a relationship with them almost as intimate as marriage. You might not want to go through this process with just anyone who happens to like the idea.

Wrapping this up

You will accumulate ideas if you take the time to write them down. At some point you do need to be objective about which idea you are going to put your effort into. This chapter was dedicated to providing you with a set of activities for doing just this task. We started with a set of techniques that can reduce the number of ideas efficiently. These are good for removing large groups of ideas that are not the right fit. The later techniques help you dig deeper and force you to confront the idea's real value.

The process can be summarized in this diagram:

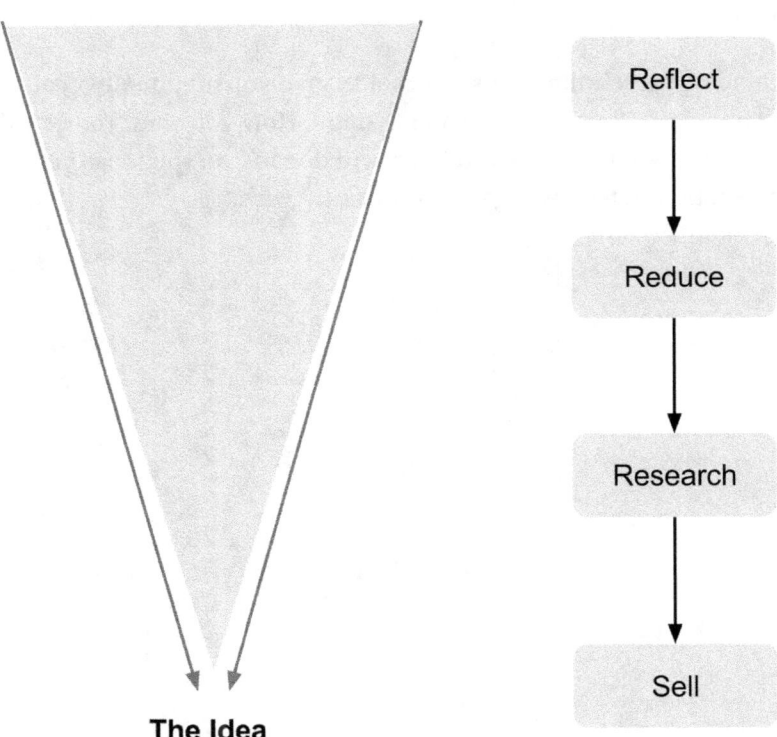

There is certainly room for new techniques that fit the right idea to the right team.

One question remains that only you can answer: When do you use this process? I suppose this comes down to your larger process for building startups. For example, you could form a team to meet and generate ideas every month. Maybe after three months you use this chapter to reduce it down to one idea and then your team is off and running. Or it could be possible that you subscribe to a philosophy in which ideas will come about organically. For instance, your team just all starts working on different ideas and as one person becomes more successful others join them. In this case the process of reduction described here would be used to help each person find an idea he or she wants to pursue.

In the end, this technique this is a tool to give you an unequivocal gut feeling about an idea that you can act upon. How you want to use this tool to fit into your culture and team will depend on the ideas you are talking about and the team you are working with.

Ideas into Businesses

Incubation

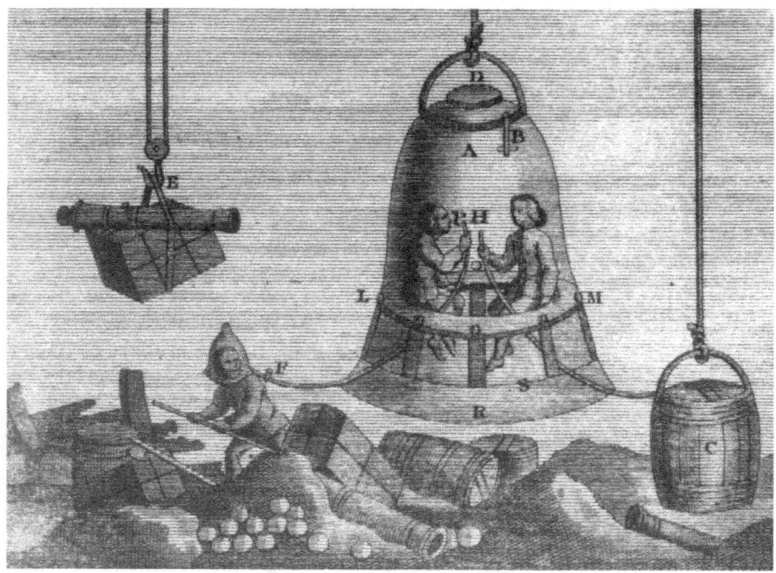

Now that you have ideas, how do you take them to the next step? This section is devoted to processes for doing just this.

Chapter 5: Ideas into Businesses

How much is an idea worth?
What is the value of an idea? There is an underlying debate in the business community related to whether ideas are really that important at all. Here is a list of the arguments I have heard.

- The team is more important. A good team can switch to a new idea easily. However, it's hard to find a new team for an old idea.

- It's not the idea that truly matters, but the problem that the idea is solving.

- The problem doesn't matters, but the *market* that the idea is addressing.

- An opportunity trumps any team, idea, or market. If you have a sale that you can close on, the idea can be altered. It is even arguable that the idea should just be thrown aside.

- If you're building a business and the idea is getting in the way, then change the idea.

So what's the point of the idea? Why even care? I assert that the idea doesn't do what most people think it does. The idea alone won't bring you success. You will need a lucky break, a team, and efficient execution of the opportunity. I doubt that even the Pet Rock idea was as simple as gluing eyes on a small rock and selling it. So the idea doesn't guarantee success. But without an idea, you can guarantee a failure.

That is because an idea is really a leadership tool. It is a way to explain your problem space, your solution, and your market in one sentence. "We are going to sell rocks with eyes to people as pets".

"We are selling groceries to people online". "We are making the best search engine possible". "We are going to put the Internet in your pocket". "We are going to bring computers to the home". All of these started as ideas and because they were this easy to communicate, a team immediately knew what they were getting into. The investors knew what was going on, the market could be sized, and the team could rally around this idea. In this case the idea acts as a sort of catalyst. It allows a leader to form his team and point them in a direction. It is your standard to rally around and you do need to be careful not just how you create it, but how you communicate it, and how you modify it along the way..

PugetWorks

Simply put, the ideas are fun, but they don't pay the bills. More importantly, I have a family who depends on me. So I started a consulting firm, PugetWorks. Originally it was just a way to make a little money as a freelance programmer, but it grew as we solved practical problems and encountered new people. That was in 2005 and so at the time of writing this book I have been running it for eight years. In that period we have seen the housing bubble crash, Obama elected, added employees, contractors, and business partners. We have seen marriages, children born, numerous medical conditions and even the occasional fatality. We have had our share of villains and heroes. On a weekly basis I've encountered problems with everything from employees with special requests, to client disagreements, to problems with money. We've had to figure out our roles, our strengths, and a multitude of solutions. I'm sure to any business owner reading this, it sounds familiar. To the rest of you, this is really just the reality of business. It's very human, very chaotic, but the accomplishments you do with your team are yours. Working as our own company we had the chance to both fail and to succeed. This constant reality seasoned our experiences and made it possible to design quickly and to reorganize when needed. At the end of the day, it was a way to "learn an MBA" and I'd recommend it for anyone.

Incubation

One aspect has remained constant throughout this journey. The plan was to sell our skills to clients and in our downtime build ventures. This is hardly unique. Many people do this by working a contract job and then building their startup on the side. What is interesting is that we focused on how to do this as a team. While some people worked, others grew the startups. This is the part that is unique and what is called a business incubator. We have attempted eight ventures already, and now we seem to be accelerating the pace.

While working on contracts for other clients we encountered all sorts of situations. Sometimes it would be a client that ran out of money, but whose idea we believe in. At other time we found an investor who liked our team and wanted to found a company together. Then there were friends who were focused on an idea and just wanted our help on it.

The point is that for the entire lifetime of PugetWorks I have been trying to make sense of how to take all of the possible scenarios that come into our office and turn them into some sort of trade that aligns everyone.

If you want to know just how complex this can be, imagine someone joining as a contractor while also being an owner to multiple ventures that we share together. So in some cases PugetWorks is the boss and in other cases the contractor is the boss. That creates a constant conflict of what this person is working on. Should the contractor be working on our mutual startup or should he be working on something else for a client? Either way it is a conflict and you can't just expect that it will resolve itself.

I think most places don't have the patience for these sort of scenarios. The underlying policy is "Do it on your own time". Many organizations want you to inform them of the intellectual property you are bringing with you to the company and the assumption is that anything you make while you are there is the company's property. The business objectives of PugetWorks were purposely muddy so that we could fully explore different social arrangements and figure out how to take an idea and turn it into a company. We needed to be in business to figure out how to bootstrap new businesses while constantly taking into account efforts from everyone. For that reason it has been rather chaotic and to all who are involved with PugetWorks, here is a hearty shout out for being pioneers.

The big question is, how do you possibly organize this so that it is fair for everyone? That is what the rest of this book is about: the processes and roles that we came up with to keep ourselves organized. This is very different from the first part of this book which was about finding and improving ideas. Now that the idea is real, we are going to implement it. So, this is a manual for organizing, taking into account real life problems.

What is 'Trade?'

No matter what you do, you must trade something. Business is trade. If you are not trading something then you are not running a business. Accepting this is key to making sure every party is aligned to the common goals of the company.

Why am I telling you this? Simply to condition your thinking to what you really need to be focused on. Up to this point you could get away with believing whatever you wanted. Trade, agreements, and compromises are the foundations of your core company and all the companies you build on top of it. So what will you be trading? What do you bring to the metaphoric table?

With every opportunity that arises, you will need to trade and figure out a deal. Every situation you have not thought of is in front of you. Sure, there are the deals you will need to make with clients, investors, partners, employees and contractors. Those are fairly straightforward after you understand how the numbers work. But what about the employee who has an idea and wants to focus on it? What about that contract that is a great product with no funding? These situations all require some sort of trade between the contributing parties.

What about working a deal with a large company? Who is going to build it? Who is going to support it? Who is going to promote it? What is all of this worth?

It will come down to the deals you put together and what you are trading in that deal. By the end of this book I will explain how we have coped with this sort of chaos.

What is a Venture?

> ven·ture /ˈvenCHər/
>
> **Noun:**
>
> A risky or daring journey or undertaking: "pioneering ventures into little-known waters".
>
> **Verb:**
>
> Dare to do something or go somewhere that may be dangerous or unpleasant: "she ventured out into the blizzard".
>
> **Synonyms noun:**
>
> hazard - adventure - risk - enterprise - gamble verb. dare - risk - hazard - adventure - chance - gamble

This was just a definition I scraped from Dictionary.com. But look at this word and think about where you would put your money. If you read this, does this sound like something you'd want to put your money on? Do you want to "invest" in a gamble? Notice in the middle of risk and gamble is the word *enterprise*.

Ideas into Businesses

I imagine that is why you are here. Probably to build a brand new business described as a "pioneering venture into little-known waters". So have you thought about exactly how much risk this will entail?

> "MEN WANTED: FOR HAZARDOUS JOURNEY. SMALL WAGES, BITTER COLD, LONG MONTHS OF COMPLETE DARKNESS, CONSTANT DANGER, SAFE RETURN DOUBTFUL. HONOUR AND RECOGNITION IN CASE OF SUCCESS. SIR ERNEST SHACKLETON"

This is the famous advertisement that Sir Ernest Shackleton used when he was recruiting for his 1914 Imperial Trans-Antarctic Expedition. I think it describes a venture quite well. I imagine that what you what you want to do isn't nearly as mortal or as gritty as what he did, but it does fall within the same definition of the word.

So why do we even do this sort of thing? Why did anyone go to Antarctica first?

I think what is important here is to think about how mortal we all really are. Not to be morose but ultimately we all have a limited number of hours that we will ever be able to put toward anything. What is even more difficult to accept is how we all have a different number and for most people for most of their lives they don't know what that number is.

I would venture to say that the first reason that someone decides to found a company that is a huge risk to their person is for the legacy that it leaves behind. We all want to try and see if we can take one of our ideas and run with it. We want to know if we were right and if we had what it takes to pull something off.

Life is constantly counting down and you have a limited amount of time to work with. Time is the driving force that makes us take on risk with imperfect knowledge. For if we knew everything, we could postpone our deaths until the engineering limits of our bodies ran out.

Now let's step out of this morbid tangent and address the second reason for starting a venture; money. I would say that this is quickly the reason for the venture after the idea is decided to be good. But, for many people money is just a justification for the experience. It is the experience of creating something to outlive us that drives us on to create a venture.

If you have children, you might suddenly realize a parallel here. In my own experience there is no greater, willing commitment of resources for an absolute unknown than my own children. What I love is that I would repeat the process no matter what, and I know that the rest of you would as well for your own. I don't want to isolate those readers who do not have children, because I imagine that you also recognize the human desire to contribute to children in ways that are logically absurd. We would all sacrifice at that level because that is who we are.

Suddenly a venture seems somewhat reasonable when put against the backdrop of an entire life.

How do we possibly bootstrap this?

Given that we now have got some ideas and the resolve to move forward with one of them, what is the plan?

The usual startup path looks something like this.

Step 1: Find an idea

Step 2: Find a co-founder with the skills you lack

Step 3: Make a pitch deck

Step 4: Find an angel investor for a seed round

Step 5: Build, measure, learn and get lucky early

Step 6: Do a VC Round A, then grow

Step 7: Do a VC Round B, then grow

Step 8: IPO or get Acquired

The alternate "lifestyle" path is

Step 1: Find an idea

Step 2: Build a low risk prototype on the side

Step 3: Pray it is successful

Step 4: If it's successful then slowly grow it until you can quit your job. Failure = GOTO Step 1

I don't know if I need to make a disclaimer here that there are other paths and the road isn't usually so simple. But this covers both ends of the spectrum in my mind. High risk, big returns and low-risk cautious growth.

For the rest of this book I'm going to propose something somewhat different from either of these paths. To be honest, I think the first one doesn't create a good business and the second one is just too slow. The first one doesn't take into account the need of a social safety net for when you fail, and the second doesn't allow for the team you need to adapt rapidly.

My proposal is for something in the middle. It is an organic pattern that I have seen emerge several time already. My hope is that after you read this next section you will suddenly start to see the same patterns. Except now, you will have a vocabulary to describe it.

Chapter 6: The Incubation Process

I love board games. Maybe it is just the aesthetics that attract me to them. What really astounds me about them, though, is that you can take a small group of adults, give them a bunch of cardboard and a set of rules, and suddenly they all take on roles that they never had up to that point. After playing the game once or twice, the players start to fill these new roles and explore what they can do within the given parameters. To me, this expresses that we can all change; it doesn't take years. It seems that it can take all of 15 minutes for the players to grasp the rules and see what the intention of the game is.

This next section should be thought of in the same way. It explains a set of roles and a process. The objective is to allow a group of people to produce one or more ventures.

The Roles

For the sake of this process there are three types of roles. Each of these roles contributes in its own way and all of them are necessary. It's possible for an individual to switch between roles within his or her group. Perhaps you are both an idea person and a contributor. You could fill all of the roles or you could find that you only like to perform one type of role. If you have a team working with you it might separate out cleanly with four people into these roles. Having said that, in my experience people have many sides to them and usually can perform all these roles, just with different degrees of skill.

Visionary

Someone must be inspired to solve a problem. Usually he or she (or you!) has been thinking about this for a while. Maybe this person was immersed in the problem or maybe the problem came back to him again and again. Slowly he put together a solution. Maybe he tried everything else available and was not able to find a solution to his liking. The point is that such people are the dreamers. They like to work on how to solve the problem. The more they talk about the idea the more excited they get about it.

Facilitator

The facilitator likes putting a team together and actually making it happen. This person forms plans, specifications, negotiates the deals and generally gets everything into workable components that can be put back together later.

The Facilitator must be able to deal with conflicts in the group and she must derive her own energy from seeing others help the idea to take shape.

Contributor

Anyone who actually contributes a skill to a project falls into this role. These are your craftsmen, designers, developers. People who get energy from doing a job and doing it well. They are proud of their skills and of the finished product and simply want some direction as to how to apply their energies most effectively.

Venture Creation Processes

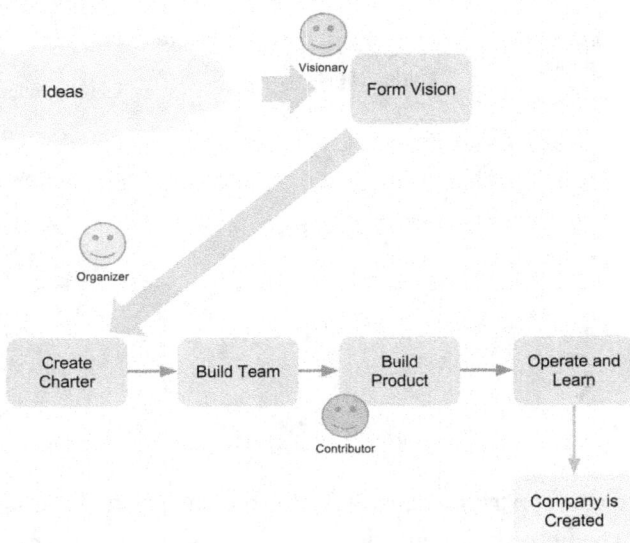

You could think of this as the game board. Ideas start on one side and come out as companies. In the middle section, the idea encounters people filling in for the different roles and carrying out different activities to grow the idea. While traveling this path, the idea changes from a simple sentence into a vision document, then into a charter document, and then into a product.

Step 1: It starts with an Idea

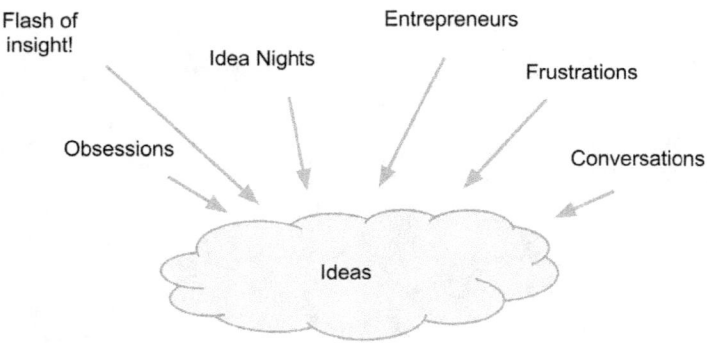

Anyone can contribute an idea. We covered several techniques already to help shake out ideas and to filter them. At this point, the idea is really just a few sentences and a name. It just points out a problem, solution, and subject matter. It should be able to fit into a sentence structured like this:

"The idea of _name_ is _40 word explanation_."

Step 2: A visionary obsesses about an idea

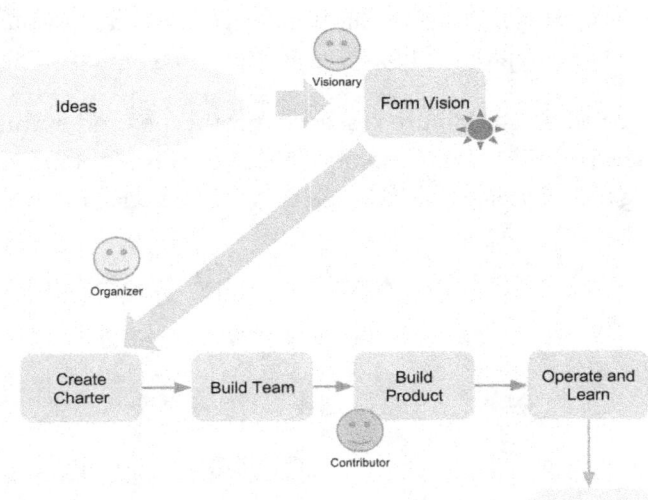

For every 50 of the ideas, probably one of them will get stuck in someone's head. That person simply cannot put it down or let it go. She keeps coming back to the problem and refining the idea. With every new technology she reads about, she tries to fit it as a solution to the problem she is obsessed with. That obsessed person is the *Visionary*.

At this point, the Visionary writes down her idea. The collection of research, arguments, features and inspiration all need to be put in one place, something I will call a *vision document*. This document gives the Visionary a place to collect her thoughts, literally. It also lets other people review those thoughts. I will cover what needs to be in the vision document more in the next chapter. For now, let's just look at it as the next stage in this process.

People work on visions in their free time. There is no pressure to "complete" a vision. Most likely the vision never will be completed for the Visionary. This is her muse, her genius, and her burden to focus on this subject for life.

As other people contribute research, prototypes and opinions to the document, it will grow. At some point it goes from being just an idea to being a *good* idea. Now it's time for a plan, hence the charter.

Step 3: The Visionary and the Facilitator create a Charter

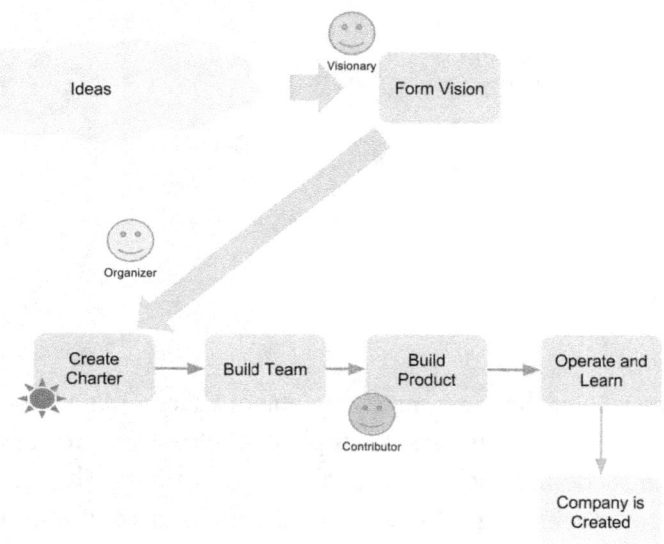

A *charter* is an actionable plan to produce a product and operate that product for a period of time. It's primary purpose is to promote learning. This needs to be a *minimum viable product,* meaning, it must satisfy this question: "What is the minimum that you have to build for someone to buy it?"

Once the product is launched, the plan must also cover who will operate it so that you can validate your assumptions about the market. You may learn that all of your assumptions are wrong. Or, instead you may learn that what you created was correct, and instead of just learning, you are making money. But the main goal is to prove that what you think about the product is true.

The real distinction between the vision and the charter is commitment. The charter is planned out and has limits; the vision document is free-formed and can go forever. Everyone involved at this point will be making a real commitment of money and/or time. So it should be written down and signed by everyone as well to symbolize their commitment.

One important detail to point out is that one vision document can have many charters. It could be that you just keep creating these and they never get executed because you can't find anyone to commit to them. This is actually a good thing, because it means that when you actually *do* get people onboard for a charter, they are all aligned as to the goal and will produce it.

I want to also emphasize that this is a huge step. Up to this point, the Visionary was most likely working alone. Having someone in the role of a *Facilitator* helping to organize and plan out is very important. This person will bring criticism to the idea and help the Visionary trim down the idea to something achievable.

Step 4: Build the Team

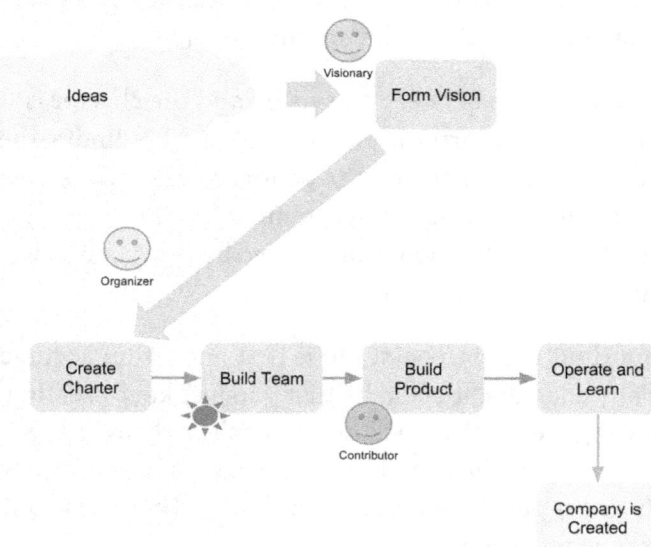

By this point in the process the idea has consisted of merely a series of papers, brainstorming, and research. It has now reached the point that there is also a concrete plan, the charter, for making this happen. Part of this charter defines the jobs and commitment needed at specific points in the creation and operation of the product. The goal now is to fill those jobs. Between the merit of the idea, the excitement of creating something new, and the potential of success, this small team must recruit its members.

Do realize that the charisma of the Visionary and Facilitator will help get people to join; however it is how well-planned and how close the team sticks to that plan that will build long-term trust. This trust is what will build your team for the long term. If you say you are going to do something and follow through with it, then other members will be much more comfortable with these ideas and promises.

Step 5: Build the Product

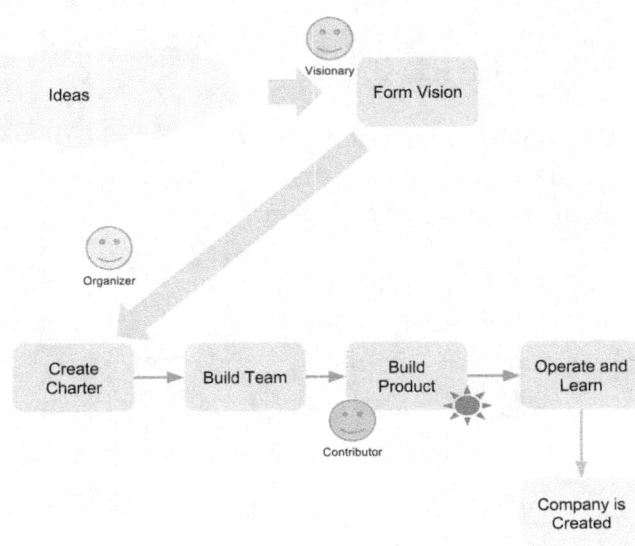

You should have a team, a plan, and an idea at this point. It is now a matter of carrying out that plan in the charter with your team to build the first version of the product. It would help if you have project management skills, but you will form them at this point. There are many books on how to do this type of task effectively so I won't go into that topic here. Be sure to look for anything about 'agile management' to help keeping the project on track.

From my own experience building product, I would recommend that you provide these three things to your team:

- A way for everyone to see what you are building, as soon as possible.

- At least a weekly meeting where you review your backlog of tasks. Focus on what has been done since the last meeting, what everyone is doing next, and what is blocking the team from making progress.

- A way to see how resources are being used on a weekly basis. Most likely this is a spreadsheet that everyone can see. It simply helps to let everyone see how close to the original plan the team has stayed.

Expect your plan to change along the way as you learn more about the technology and team. This step is all about building; incidentally, it is one of my favorite parts of the process.

Step 6: Operate and Learn

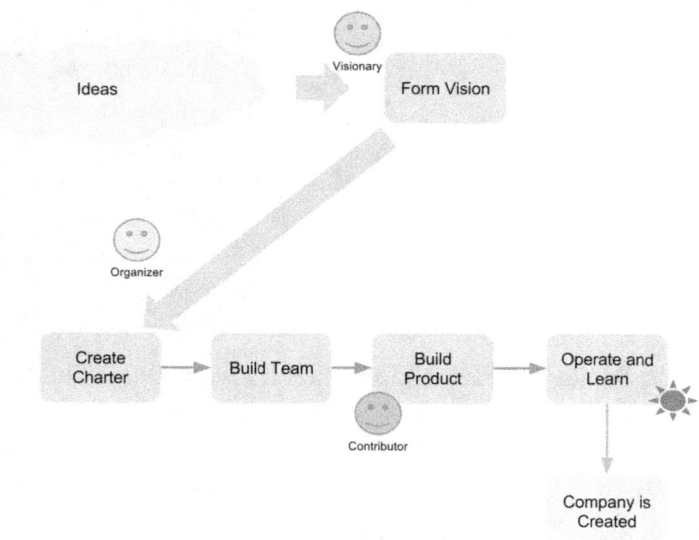

Finally your product is done and your team is focused on operating the product. This could mean that they are fulfilling orders or just making sure that someone can use it. I won't go into this phase in a huge amount of detail because Eric Ries covers it very well in his book *Lean Startup*. I would highly recommend that you read this book and be aware of the enormous amount of information that has formed around this subject.

The general idea is that you select meaningful metrics to determine how your product or service is performing. You then track these metrics while you try altering features. You should also be talking to your customers and learning about their problems. All of this information helps you build a product or service that someone wants to use.

You may discover that what you built isn't quite useful in the way you originally thought, but could be made useful with slight modifications. That is called a *pivot*, when you start over on the product based on what you have learned. To fit to the process I'm describing here, that pivot could merit a new charter or it could be planned into the original charter. As long as it is clear to your Contributors how this will work then you should have a lot less frustration if you suddenly realize you have to start over.

Step 7: Company is Created

This step is somewhat ambiguous because it could have happened at any point along this path. By "creating" a company, I mean that you have filed it with the government and have all the necessary licenses. So now you have a taxable entity that is in the form of an LLC, C-Corp, or S-Corp. With that change comes percentage ownership and a responsibility to report income to the government for tax purposes.

I list this as the last step because at some point you must actually form an organization in the formal manner. I would advise that you push this off until it is absolutely necessary. This could take the form of needing a working bank account for funds, or needing an entity for setting up accounts. I would argue that as soon as money become part of the product or service, then you must have a company set up. This could begin as far back as when you're recruiting a team or building the product. Doing this is a bit of work, but it is one of the most concrete steps along the way. There are also plenty of books and professionals that can help you out with this part.

The reason to postpone filing the company is simple: the longer you wait, the more you understand your team and everyone's contribution. This information could heavily influence how many shares everyone has in the company. If you file it early you must deal with the challenge of guessing how everything will work out, balanced against what is fair.

If you can wait until this point, then do so. Remember that you are not just trying to make a company, but a company that can last for a long time. Dealing with feelings of unfairness and tension will help after the team has been working together building trust.

Conclusion

Working your way through this process requires a different set of skills at every point. You could almost think of every step of the process as wrapping the idea in another layer. The end result might look something like this:

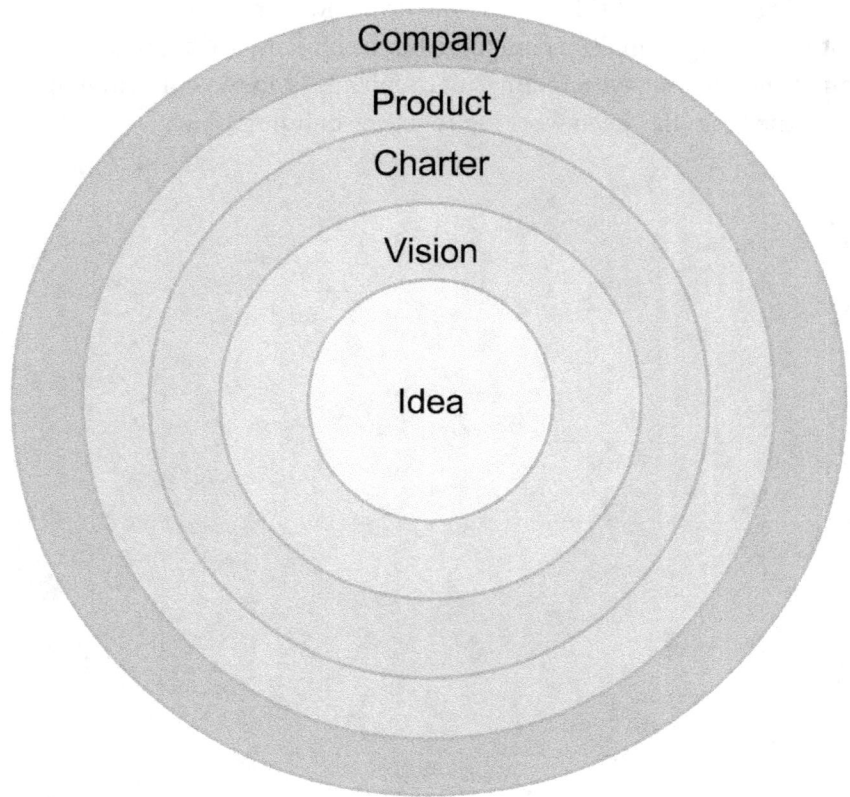

Buried in the middle of a company is an idea that started it all. The rest of this book is devoted to covering different aspects of this process in more detail. This was the first pass to introduce the roles and the game board upon which everything else will be built.

Chapter 7: The Vision and the Charter

Two Modes of Thinking

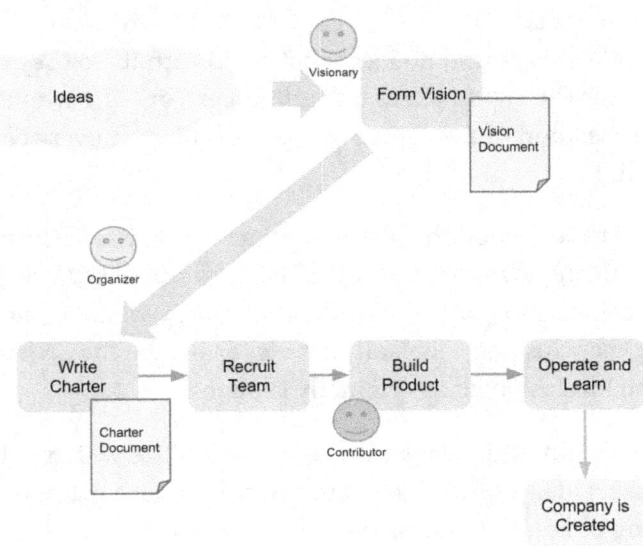

In the previous chapter we talked about the path that an idea takes as it forms into a company. Along the way a vision document and charter document are to be created. These two activities are key for the transition of growing an idea, and it could take years to get through this phase.

Originally, I thought that a business plan would be the right tool for bridging this gap. But a business plan is used more for explaining why you want to be financed and for making an argument that you can pay back whomever loaned you money. These two documents should help you focus on the two mindsets you will need to build out your company. One is for dreaming, and the other is for action. Keep this in mind when you are building any venture. If you are not sure which phase you're in, you're in a dreaming phase.

Which phase are you in?

It is most important that you recognize which phase you are in: Are you in the laid-back experimenter phase? Or are you in the driven, get-it-done phase? It's easy to confuse these two. Some startups start with a pile of cash and no idea what to do with it. So they charge off looking for the right idea to burn their cash on. The whole time, they realize they don't have a plan for success. I have never seen this work out well.

At other times, when the opportunity presents itself, the plan may be ready, but the team is not. Maybe they never will be. Maybe there are better things going on around them that they would rather work on. Maybe the wins don't look all that big, or maybe they really aren't into the idea as much as originally thought.

Acknowledging this reality allows you to realize which of these phases the idea is in and to commit resources accordingly. If it's the thinking phase, then it's okay to be experimenting with different business models. In this phase, it's fine to be trying out technologies and researching at leisure. But this sort of thing should always be done in the background. These are activities for evenings, weekends, and downtime. This is not when you want to be burning capital on these activities. I call this the "Vision" phase and it comes with the relaxed cadence of play.

Then there is the 'doing' phase. This is when the plan has been acknowledged; now it's time to take some risks. People might leave their jobs, companies can budget real resources, investors can get involved. This is when we have something ready to go and it's time to make things happen. I call this the 'charter' phase and it involves planning then acting on that plan.

Separating out the mindsets into these two different ways of thinking is very important for keeping everyone aligned as to what is happening. You don't want someone to take big risks before the rest of the team. You don't want to be the only person taking risks. You don't want to ignore your paying clients on a whim. But you do want to go fast and build what you need to, when you need to. Deciding this moment is an art and requires patience and guts.

Writing it down

When you are in the 'experimentation' phase, create a "Vision" document. Before you build the idea, create a "Charter" document. The "Vision" document will record all of your research, ideas, and inspiration. The "Charter" document will contain your plan for when things need to be done, what features are necessary and the details of making this happen.

It should be noted that one Vision document might spawn multiple Charters. Perhaps two teams like the idea, but want to take it in different directions. Perhaps you try with the first Charter and fail, but want to try again with another Charter. The idea may live forever, even if the projects that attempt to implement it fail. The hope is that the collective knowledge of these attempts pools into the Vision document so that the next person will start from this point.

The rest of this chapter is devoted to explaining what the sections of each document are and why they are important. It is broken into sections, each of which is there to create conversation in your team and to help you look at the idea from a different perspective.

Finally, I want to make a point that this is, and always will be, a work in progress. There will be new sections that are thought of that will help shed new light on a vision or a charter.

The Vision Document

Simply put, the vision document lets you elaborate on the idea without getting caught up in the details. It doesn't imply a commitment or any actual work. It is for the dreamer and the visionary to mull the idea over, to grow it and add to it. This is in stark contrast to the charter, which is a concrete plan that is to be executed upon. Both are necessary; but always start here.

Important: Efforts Log

The Effort Log is a tool for trust and it conveys how much effort has been put into the project. When someone tells you her idea, it is very hard to tell if she just came up with it on the way over or if she has been working on it for years. It could be the third version of the idea after two previously failed startups. You simply don't know. So in this section we create a log of the amount of time that has been put into an idea. Originally, I thought this log should be expressed in financial terms. But, the reality is that cost is a function of time. This venture will have people who invest their time and people who invest their money, so it's important to reduce things to a common variable for all involved. Time is the only constant that puts everyone on an equal basis.

Now there are a couple things to consider here: For one, if you put money into the idea, you need to reach consensus as to what that means. There should be an hourly rate or a set of hourly rates that can be used to relate someone's time to someone else's money. This should be documented somewhere and only changed if everyone affected agrees. Simply changing this rate can be a major game-changer, one that alters the balance of fairness. So pick a rate carefully and stick to it as much as you can. The people putting money into the idea want to know that they are being treated fairly as much as the people putting in time.

There's one other corner case: What about the people who contribute *opportunity*? What if they have some connection or a situation that can make the project a success - what is that worth? I would advise that you estimate the amount of time it would take to get a similar connection or situation and use that value. And just as if you were working out a story problem for a high school math teacher, show your work. For the team to become a team, everyone must trust everyone else. If they can see how the others are thinking that will happen a lot faster. So back up your assumptions. You may have fewer or more hours than you wanted from this exercise, but if this forms a stronger team and increases success then everyone will get past this.

What this 'efforts section' really does is bring an uncomfortable conversation to the beginning instead of having a very uncomfortable conversation at the end. At some point everyone will have a grievance about some perceived unfairness or misunderstanding. I highly advise that you follow this practice so that you have these conversations *before* someone joins the project instead of thousands of hours later, when it really matters.

Important: Concept Drawing

Nothing communicates better than a picture. Every idea needs one. It doesn't have to be the actual artist composition of what the product will look like. But, it needs to be that one picture that really shows why this idea is cool. What gets you excited about it? It could be a picture of someone simply using it or how it could save the day. Maybe it is the vision that sticks in your head when you came up with the idea. It simply needs to have an emotional response. Most likely the response you want is, "Yeah!".

I wouldn't really focus on the problem the idea is solving. That is more of a negative way to show the same thing. But, it gets people caught up in the wrong emotion. You want this to get them jazzed about the idea. So stick to a picture of how it will make someone feel to use the app. Maybe a picture of the app solving the problem. If you do this right, you can capture the problem and the solution in one image.

You see, in the first part you showed how much work has been put into this idea; in this part you want to evoke an emotional response. This lets people sample the idea and size up the effort in a single glance.

Important: Idea Description

Now it's your chance to pitch your idea to your readers. To write this section, simply answer the questions. Questions are a fantastic way to create a conversation with your readers, so this section is structured as a dialogue. The questions are meant to not let you talk their ears off, but to get the most relevant information in front of them so they can decide what they think about your idea.

One thing to note: don't get too wordy. Beauty here is in being concise. If you ramble you will lose focus. There are larger sections later for breaking out feature sets, business models and other things; this is to give someone some details into the visionary's thinking process. They are deciding if they want to join this team and this section will help them make that decision.

1. What is the elevator pitch?

What is the slogan or the mantra? These are simple sentences that explain where you are trying to take the idea.

2. Where did you think of the idea?

Give the backstory. Everyone loves to know the origin story and where this idea came from. It makes working on it more compelling.

3. What problem does it solve?

Is this problem even relevant? Is it still a problem? This lets everyone understand the visionary's level of focus. It also might be adjusted because your idea might solve a much larger problem than what you originally started focusing on.

4. What represents success for this idea?

You don't have to describe this with a massive amount of detail, but you do have a chance here to elaborate on your vision of success. Does it mean making money from building a solid business? Do you want to solve world hunger? Do you want to have this outfit get acquired?

5. What *won't* this idea do?

This is your chance to clarify the things you don't want this idea to deal with. Maybe you don't want it to be confused with a different product. Maybe you keep getting comments from people to the effect of "oh this is already done and it's this other project". *You* know, however, that this isn't even the same market. This is your chance to form a blacklist of what you are not doing.

Important: Reactions

There should always be a space for your readers to provide feedback to the vision. I would suggest that you structure this as a list with each commenter's name, a simple letter grade and a description. It keeps it simple when a future reader scan the reactions that the idea received.

Don't get too hung up on what grades other readers give your idea. Success here isn't having the perfect idea. It's having an idea that attracts a team. No one will know if the idea has any value until you start to learn your customers' reactions to it. You will never get there if you don't have a team, so that is your starting point.

Also note that when people contribute, they are part of your team. So don't feel discouraged when someone behaves critically toward the venture. Many people will mentally join on to an idea and then immediately start trying to fix it by pointing out its problems. When it is your idea it is easy to take this personally and feel like they are criticizing *you*.

You need to separate yourself from this. Instead, realize that when someone starts to criticize they are actually *joining* you. This is a good thing. Don't fear the debate, but justify your thinking; it will only make your idea stronger. Also, the more other people debate with you, the more they have contributed to the idea. Pretty soon you will have a team.

Suggested: Customer Profiles and Assumptions

This is possibly the most important section: defining who your customer is with regards to this idea. You see, an idea by itself is just a thought that is fun to tell people about. But when it really starts to become a business is when you figure out who you are going to trade with. You need to really spell this out.

- Who is going to want this?
- What sorts of persons are they?
- What are the problems they are having?

You may find that you have more than one customer profile. This is ok. When you finally build something you need to start with just the most likely customer profile. But until then, you need to be listing your assumptions and trying to figure out how true these assumptions are.

Suggested: Potential Business Models

Once you know who the customers of this idea would be, you need to spell out how you would make money from them. What is the trade? In its simplest form, this is what business is all about: trading something. So for each of these potential customer types the trade could be wildly different.

- Do you plan on selling this person one thing, one time only?
- Do you plan on giving something away and having them pay for more later?
- Do you plan on offering a service?
- How much will all of this cost?
- What are the parameters around this trade? Duration?

List these different ways here so that your team can review your thinking. It might even be smart to survey your different customer profiles to see if these numbers would work.

One tool I would point out is something called a "lean canvas". This came about from the Lean Startup movement based on the book Lean Startup by Eric Ries. A lean canvas is a one page business plan and at the time of writing this there were some great websites that walk you through the process. The end result is something that looks like a placemat that helps you think about how you would sell this idea and who would want it.

Suggested: Competitive Analysis

As soon as you tell someone the idea, inevitably that person will bring up someone who is already doing this. Here is a section to keep track of these groups.

Explain how these groups align with or differ from your effort. Explain how they are likely (or not) to make money, if you can discern their methods. One thing you shouldn't do with this section is to get discouraged. Too many times I have seen engineers give up as soon as something similar to their idea shows up. The belief seems to be that if it has already been done once then, then it's not worth attempting again. It's true that being first has some advantages, but only in the beginning.

For the most part you should view competitors as a good indicator that there is something worth pursuing in this space. Most importantly, you should be trying to figure out when this market will be ready for your product. If you get there too early, then there will not be enough customers. If you get there too late, then all the margins will be shrinking and the product is being commoditized. You need to figure out if you are still in that nice window in the middle. Tracking your competitors will help.

Remember the market wave picture from earlier in the book?

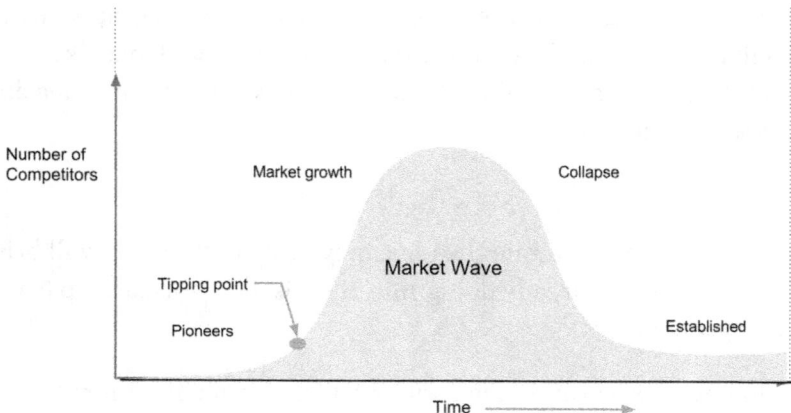

This is an illustration of the same thing. But it is very hard to figure out where you are on this wave. You want to be surfing the front, not the back and one way to tell is to get a feel for what others are doing in the same space and how they are succeeding.

Suggested: Potential Ownership Structures

Ownership is a big deal when it comes to a venture. What isn't always clear is how the rewards will be shared. When I started doing this, I thought it was only about shares and what part of the pie I would get. In an ideal state it is that simple. But ownership comes with responsibilities. You can't expect every person to be as committed or to think like you.. So instead, you need to engineer a structure of ownership with your founders and the people who will be joining you later.

We will cover this in detail in a later chapter, but this is where you can list ownership structures that could happen. It is important to explain that there may be several deals that show up here. When you actually form a charter you will pick one of these.

Suggested: Risks and Fears

At some point you must be realistic about the idea. Denial of the obvious problems only ruins your credibility with those following your vision. There will also be dark moments when you look at this idea and say to yourself, "This is stupid". Fear is irrational, but it might not be unfounded. Best to list your concerns here and then confront them.

You might learn that your fears are shared by the rest of the group. Maybe by figuring out a clever solution you can mitigate those fears. In the end if you have removed all the fears and shown a fantastic reward, then it is time to create your charter and go. But, it will be the fears of the group that hold it back. So think of this section as your 'fuse,' so to speak.

Suggested: Potential Technology Solutions

This is a section for technical people. Sometimes it is the technology that makes the idea. Just seeing some new sort of light bulb or gadget inspires us to want to use it. Maybe it is so cool that it actually replaces a previous problem you had been considering. I would like to point out that this glow will wear off and then it's back to the art of crafting a business. Even so, we should list this technology somewhere. If it inspires us it is important to let that inspiration keep us interested.

Suggested: Research

Finally, while you explore your ideas you will encounter lots of articles that are interesting and somewhat relevant. This section is a dumping ground for such information. It is at the bottom of the document for a reason. It is really just a listing of bookmarks and citations that will help give history or context to the vision.

The Charter Document

In running and growing a software consultancy, I have had to create hundreds of proposals. Every proposal has parts that make it completely unique, but they all pull from a common thread. First, someone explains their situation, the technologies, and the backstory and where they plan on going. I talk about who we are, and if it seems like a match I create a proposal for this potential client.

My proposals are not elaborate. They focus on how much work we should budget for to get this client to where they want to go. I focus on what type of people would be needed at what point and how many hours they would use. Usually I break it all down by week and specify if each person involved would be working a full week or some percentage of the week. These proposals take me about an hour to think through; at the end of the process I propose a plan that includes the number of people, a timeline, and a cost.

The Charter document is a plan for creating an MVP (*minimum viable product*) and budgeting time to work with that MVP through one or more pivots. It gives your team an idea as to what you expect to happen and what the result of this will be so they can decide if they want to join you.

By the way, if you're unfamiliar with the term "minimum viable product", then you need to read the book *Lean Startup* by Eric Ries. It has become the definitive guide to building a start-up company. Several of the principals in this book are built on concepts from *Lean Startup*. In my opinion, the most important concept is that of the Minimum Viable Product. Ries, does a great job of explaining this in depth, but to summarize: "What is the least you have to do to get someone to pay you for your product or service?"

Now Ries isn't saying you shouldn't take pride in what you're building. His point is that you shouldn't keep adding on new features that someone might not pay for. Do the minimum, do it well, and don't stress out about scalability. You just have to sell it; then you can grow it.

This is what the charter document is about. You are now going to take all the thoughts in your head about your idea and turn them into an actionable plan.

One thing to point out is that this is always a work in progress. This Charter should be reviewed periodically to make sure you are on track for what you said you were going to do.

Important: Vision Document Reference

Provide a reference to the vision document so that readers can learn the background behind the idea.

Important: Ownership

Contributor	Ownership	Why?
Person 1 person1@company.com	49%	Researched the idea for 5 years
Person 2 person2@company.com	49%	Responsible for building the system
Advisor1 advisor1@company.com	2%	Advisor moving forward

Create a table describing how ownership will be apportioned and for what reasons. You may want to use strategies later in this book to explain this part. But, you need to state who owns what percentages.

It could also be that you are talking about a revenue split or convertible debt. List those types of trades here so everyone knows what is going on. Even if the company isn't filed for six months, at least everyone knows what their stake is in this project.

Important: Debt Tracking

You should track how much time and cost are put into the project in this section. Explain what is considered 'debt' and what that means for the company. Does it mean it needs to be paid back? Is this debt part of the ownership arrangement? Consider this a ledger where your team can keep track of how resources are used.

Important: Ultimate Goal

State what the goal for this project is. Is it to merge, go IPO, be a lifestyle business, solve a altruistic problem? What represents 'success' for your idea? The reason this is important is that anyone contributing needs to have this same goal.

Important: Plan

Break down your plan into three-month phases and explain how many hours you expect to use in each phase. You need to give an idea of the skills that will be required for each phase and what the goal is for each one. What happens if you don't achieve these goals?

I would also urge you to focus on which phases are intended for *creating* something and which phases are planned for *operating* what you've created.

Suggested: Customer Section

Targeted Customer Profiles
At this point you need to choose the customer profile from your vision document and call it out here. Remember that you should only be dealing with the minimum number of customers to ultimately charge one of them. So you could end up with more than one profile in this section. For instance, you might have a user and an advertiser.

Don't forget that you should also be listing all of your assumptions with each profile. Some of these you may have validated earlier, but you must figure out what you know and don't know about these customers.

Customer Metrics

How will you validate your customer assumptions with your product? What sort of "funnel" will they need to go down so you can see where you are losing them? What can you track to know if your assumptions are correct?

These are all questions you need to figure out and later build a spreadsheet around. You will periodically need to be watching what the users of your product/service are doing to figure out if some of your assumptions were wrong about your customers. Once again I reference *Lean Startup* and you should read more about it there. However, this is the place on your charter to list this type of information.

Engine of Growth

This is another concept from *Lean Startup*. The question is "How will new customers find out about you?". Eric Ries describes three broad strategies that I paraphrase below. You should try to stick to one of these.

Sticky Engine of Growth

This engine relies on having a high customer retention rate. You should be tracking how many new customers you are getting versus how many are leaving. These variables are known as the *acquisition rate* and the *attrition rate*. You can also figure out how long customers are staying with your product or service from this.

Viral Engine of Growth

In this case, customers do the marketing for you. They usually either tell friends about your product or service explicitly, or they market it simply by using it. To determine if you are growing you will need to track how many new customers come with each existing one. This becomes your *viral coefficient* and the average of it needs to be greater than one.

Paid Engine of Growth
For this engine of growth to work you will be paying for each customer who joins your system. What you will need to be tracking is the *Cost per Acquisition* (CPA) and the *Lifetime Value* (LTV) of each customer. The margin between this LTV and CPA represents how quickly your company is growing.

Suggested: Scope Definition

User Stories
User stories are a concept that comes from software engineering. It's a sentence that describes who would want to use your product and why. By listing them out you can concisely explain all the different types of people who would use a system like this and for what purposes. To create one you simply fill in the blanks.

As a __ I want to ___ so that I can ___ because ___

For instance if you were to describe Google with a user story you might say:

> As a **user** I want to **search the Internet** so that I can **find things I need** because **there are too many places to know about.**

It is very important to note that you should have several of these sentences describing your product. What these really do is describe why this product should exist and who would be served by it.

Feature set
After you have gone through the user stories you are starting to get a feel for the features in this system. Start writing them down, preferably in a bulleted list. Once you have all of these features in one place, organize them.

Which of these features must be in the core version? Which features would be nice to have but could come online in version 2? Which features are really cool but could be put off until some time in the future?

What you are trying to do here is limit the scope. In lean startup terms you want a minimum viable product or MVP. The guiding principle here is this:

What is the least you have to create for a customer to pay you?

That should determine your first set of features.

Technology and Tools

Whatever you are planning on building, it will be made out of something (even bits, if we're talking about software). What will you need to create this product? What supporting tools are required?

For some people the technology is central to the product. In many cases they simply got the idea by looking at a new technology and applying it to an old problem. Thus the technology should be called out as a cornerstone to this solution.

Another key reason to get this in front of all stakeholders is that it might be over-thought. A product should not just be an exciting use of a novel technology. It should provide value to an end customer.

Suggested: Project Management Section

Timeline

Starting here, you need to list all of your key dates and why you've chosen them. This is going to determine lots of things for your project. Below I've listed several dates that you should make sure to lock down:

Date	Why?
January, 1, 20??	Kickoff
April, 1, 20??	MVP Completion Date
August, 1, 20??	Sales Goal 1
December, 31, 20??	Kill Date

Schedule

This is where you really map out a concrete plan for when things need to get done to form this charter. It will quickly let you figure out what the required skill sets are and for how long they'll be required. This is also a very easy section to review. In many cases people do not know how to break this part down, but you will need to try and to review it with others, if only so that you can have this sort of experience. Keep in mind one thing: everything will always take longer than you thought. So don't be too optimistic. This is an art, not a science, and the principles of Agile Project Management can help you to form a team to work through the feature backlog thought through earlier.

The questions you should ask are:

- *How long will our sprints be?*
- *How many sprint cycles do we need to create this?*
- *What are the first features to work through?*

After that, you'll need to figure out what life will be like when you are operating this product or service:

- *What sorts of people need to be involved to create this product or operate this service?*

- *How many hours a week do you estimate they will need to do these jobs?*

- *How long will you be running this service?*

Jobs

Based on the schedule for building this and running it you now have a fairly good idea for the types of people you need involved and what you expect from them. From this you can create several job requirements or "job reqs". These should address the following:

- *When would you need to be involved?*

- *When are you done?*

- *How much effort do we expect from you?*

- *What will you get for this?*

Suggested: Sales Section

Marketing Strategy

Depending on your engine of growth this might be very important. For instance if you are using a "paid engine" of growth, then it will come down to paying people to get new customers. But in all cases you will need to get the word out somehow. How will this work? The following questions will help fill out this section:

- *How will you tell new customers about you?*

- *Will there be press releases?*

- *Who is responsible for telling people about your product or service?*
- *How will you target your customers?*

Business Model

Since you are building a minimum viable product one of the requirements is that you can sell it. So what will you charge for this? Your business model describes what you are going to sell and how you will price it. It's vital to figure this out early on even if you completely change it later on.

The questions you need to answer are:

- *What am I selling?*
- *Are there discounts?*
- *Are there any warranties?*
- *How will you charge your customers?*
- *Will your customers need to sign a contract? If so, what would it look like and what are the legal implications?*

Sales Plan

If you are building a company that will be low volume and high margins you might need to consider your sales staff. Do you need people to be ready to take a call and talk to a potential customer? What sort of "sales funnel" will you have? If you are building a B2C web app this might be completely irrelevant. You simply charge credit cards and never meet your customer.

If you ever have to talk to your customers before they pay you, then you will have someone in the role of sales. If moving this product has anything to do with answering questions, explaining a process, or setting expectations, then you need to train these people and arm them with the right information.

These people might also need ways to make demos, and do presentations. But all of this can be sorted out. The main thing you need to figure out is how you will incentivize them. Here are a series of questions you need to answer:

- *How do you plan on selling this?*
- *Who will be responsible?*
- *Will a commission be involved?*
- *How will the commission work?*
- *Will they have 'territories?'*
- *How many of these people will you need?*

Suggested: Financing Section

Finally, every plan needs this section. It shows that you are actually trying to balance risk and reward. It is arguably the core of your business. After you have filled out all the other sections, fill this one out.

Budget

This really breaks down to two things: What will this cost to build and what will this cost to operate? The trick here is that you have to assume that everyone is a contractor and working on an hourly rate. I will go into detail on this point later, but what it boils down to is that at this point in your project everyone is putting time into your project as an investor. So treat everyone the same. You can optimize this later by hiring people and maybe getting lower market rates. But you need to be able to really look at this and say, "Is it worth $500k worth of time to get this built?".

So the questions you must answer are these:

- *What will this cost to build?*
- *How much will this cost every month to run?*

It would be good to get as detailed as possible here because these guesses will be tested fairly rapidly, and it will be good to see where you are wrong earlier rather than later.

Investments Pledged

It's conceivable that someone wants to help out financially. In such a case, you need to find out how much this person is willing to contribute and how quickly he could bring his money to the table.

Also, as soon as possible you need to file paperwork on your company. No one wants to just give you money without getting something in return. You will be able to choose between giving them shares or convertible notes. Stick to shares if you can both agree on the price and use convertible notes if you cannot agree on what the company is worth.

Either way, write down your handshake agreement here. After you kick off this project you can collect on this pledge.

Projections

This section is your dessert for getting through everything else. Projections are really just fun and mostly to cheer the founders up. Since thinking through and discussing all of this is the hard part you need to have this in here; just save it until last. I don't think anyone investing time or money expects it to be right, but it is just fun to make a hockey stick graph.

Basically, crack open your spreadsheet and put in the next five years. Put in the numbers that tell how much this will cost and how much you will make. Set this up with some variables so you can see what it would look like with different retention rates and pricing models. If you do it just right, you can sometimes show that you will make all the money in the world in the next five years.

After you feel like you have come up with something realistic, paste a picture of the graph here. Years later you can all grin at it as you have something more realistic to show. But, in the meantime it is a fun diversion and a good way to boost your spirits.

Conclusion

One problem with both the visionary and the vision is that they usually are very one-sided. They have focused on the parts they enjoy the most. Either it's all about the people who will be helped, how awful the problem is, or how cool the technology would be. But, building a new company is extremely hard and no one does it alone. It starts as a conversation in your head and slowly expands to become a conversation with your partners. Then it becomes a conversation with your financiers, then with your employees. Finally, you are conversing with your customers. It's really a long-winded negotiation between an unknown number of individuals to form a pattern that they can all be successful within. They call it an *organization* for a reason.

When other people get involved in the vision for the idea, it will start to round out. Suddenly all of those uncomfortable, non-interesting parts of the idea will need addressing. This happens as soon as you try to communicate the vision to others - most likely because at this point you either are asking for a financial partner to fund it, or a technology partner to build it with.

So questions will be asked, and the visionary addresses them, altering the idea as she goes. She finds flaws and makes adjustments. Maybe she learns about competitors and understands the market better as a result. Maybe she starts to add or trim features. It really depends on who is looking at this and what his or her individual experience is.

In my experience, there is a time for conversations such as the following:

- What are we selling?

- How many people would want to buy this?

- Are the number of people buying this increasing?

- Why would they want to buy this and not that?
- What do we make it out of?

Notice that this series of questions are very different from:

- What should I work on today?
- Who is going to fix that?
- How do I pay that guy?

The first set defines your company, the second set represents work that just needs to get done. But when you have time on your side, it's that first set that you should be working on; that way, when you do suddenly start moving forward, these questions will already be answered. Granted, validating these answers is what the business is all about. Just don't wait until you press the launch button to figure them out.

This chapter helped provide a foundation for the questions and aspects of the idea you will need to think through. Next we will show how this plays out over time.

Chapter 8: The Life of an Idea

In the previous chapter we introduced the Vision document and the Charter. In this chapter we will describe how these different parts work together.

Let's start by revisiting the diagram from earlier.

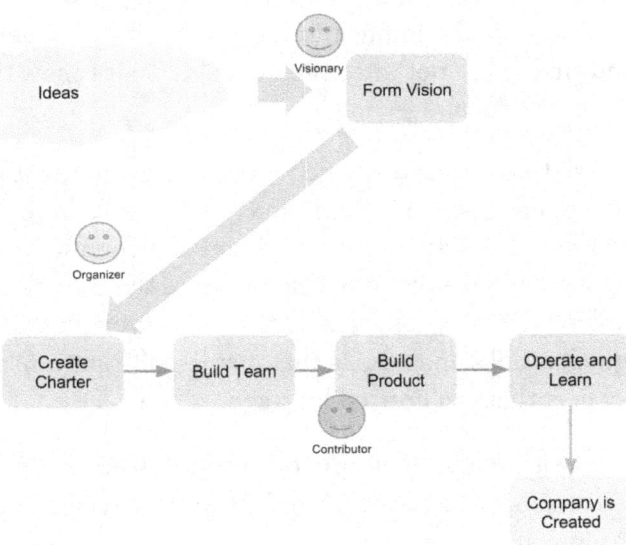

The journey begins with the idea. From the previous chapters we have talked about how these ideas form and how we might go about filtering them. They could stay in this state forever. Most ideas are really not worth very much. I think the joke is that it cost somewhere between a "penny for your thoughts" and a "dime a dozen". Thus the ideas at this point are worth somewhere between 1 cent and .83 cents.

However some ideas simply will not leave us alone. They haunt us and we can't stop thinking about them. Personally, I have found that I can become obsessed with an idea; after three days if it still is hanging on in my mind, I create a vision document for it.

That's the next step: to start putting some effort into it. Create a vision document somewhere and start filling in the sections. As you start committing more time to the idea, you will begin to refine your vision. It might be that you discover that you really are not that into this project. Perhaps it just doesn't resonate with you after all. Maybe having the 'first mover advantage' is something you really wanted. Maybe you realize the implications of the business model you would need and simply are not interested enough. So it is now time to take a break from this idea.

Now realize that at this time the vision document might just sit there. You might come back to it from time to time and add to it, maybe pine over how great an idea it is and how someone should build it. You might even have that day when you see that someone else did it and think to yourself, "oh, well". Maybe then you play with what the other guy has built and realize that it still isn't right. He's missing that key part that *you* noticed long ago.

So the idea sits on a shelf, until you encounter some money, a co-founder, or simply just a long chunk of time. Maybe something happens in your life and you say, "let's do this". You find that you don't want to wait around forever to find out that you were right.

That's when the charter really begins. Now you're ready to commit. So you create the Charter and start to recruit. With every recruit comes another review of your idea. And with every review it gets stronger and more realistic. Now other people are starting to see what you are seeing.

The charter looks solid, the team is on board, so you pick a kick-off date and execute on the plan. Now everyone knows where they are going and what they need to do. You have aligned the team so that expectations are set properly.

The product goes live and you are now in the world of lean startup following the *build, measure, learn* lifecycle. If you manage this part correctly, then your company is formed and your idea has been proven worthwhile, so now you are making money and you know longer need this book.

I would consider this the "happy path" for how everything could work. I don't think it is completely unrealistic, but it is just one one of the stories that can unfold from how the idea is formed and executed on.

This chapter describes what could happen at key points when you fall off the happy path. More importantly, it details what happens to all that effort you put into the idea.

What if your idea wasn't that great?

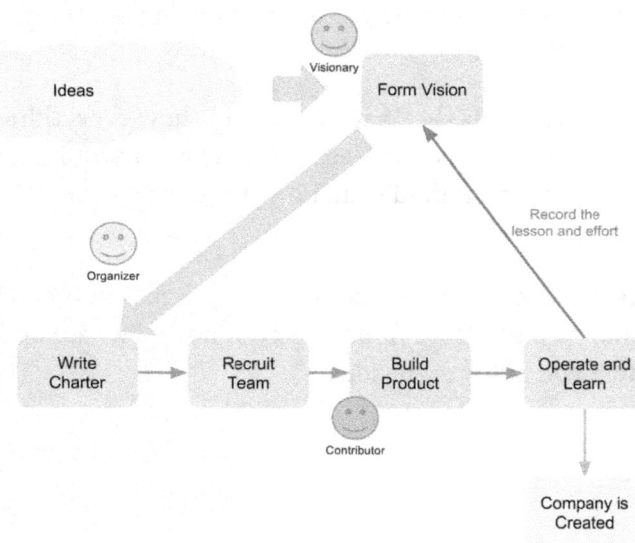

What if you are wrong? What if you reach the kill date and it turns out that the idea just cannot get traction with your original product? You could pivot, but really your team isn't into it anymore. For that matter, maybe something happened in your life and you don't really want to do this anymore. Or maybe a better idea presented itself. Is it time to give up? Yes, but don't throw all that learning away. Write down what you did, what you learned, into the Vision document at least.

That is the point really: As one of my friends put it, "experience is what you get when you don't get what you want". So instead of lamenting it, cut your losses and move on.

I think that this trap of wasted effort happens to everyone. If you put one hour into something, can you walk away? Sure, no big deal; it was just an hour. What about one *year* of your life? That will certainly be more difficult. But if you come to the conclusion that this was not the right path and you have a better alternative, it makes the most sense to cut your losses and move on. I think this might be one of the hardest decisions ever to make: to give up something you are not happy or excited about, but have put part of your life into, in order to pursue something totally unknown.

Thus this process provides an escape valve for just this situation. Take a break from the idea, let it bake, write it down, and move on.

What could happen next is that you give it some time and then try again. A new charter gets created and the cycle starts all over again. With each pass through this cycle, more is learned.

If you are really being haunted by a muse and it won't let you get away from the idea, then you will have a chance to try again.

What if you cannot find a co-founder?

Are you an "Idea Person"? Do you prefer to read about new, fantastic things and predict the future? Maybe you really get excited about what is coming next and have all of these great thoughts on how to get there. If so, you are a Visionary. Maybe you can be described as "having your head in the clouds." If you follow this process you will find out pretty quickly that you have a pile of vision documents and no charters.

However, maybe you are a different type of person. You have a yearning to build something that you own. Maybe you long to lead a team of people toward something better, but you don't quite know where to start. You just have this fire in you that will not go out. In this case you are a leader. If you didn't know that until this moment, then this is the time to finally accept it. You want to be in charge because you can do a better job, because you are organized, or because you just like helping figure out how people fit together to form a team.

It could be that you are the type of person who wants to participate in bringing one of these ideas to life. You don't necessarily have a vision that you are obsessed with, and you don't feel a need to lead something. You don't necessarily care what it is, but the medium, the team and the tools matter the most. You are a craftsman who wants to be proud of the work you do. All you want from your comrades is for them to give it their all so that you can all look back afterward and bask in the glow of a job well done. If this describes you, then you are a Contributor.

This creates a problem, though: How do you find the people that you want to work with? How do you even know what your options are?

The answer is that there are two additional parts missing from our system. These are: a) the *idea market* where leaders can look for visionaries; and b) the *charter market* where other members can look for opportunities.

The Idea Market

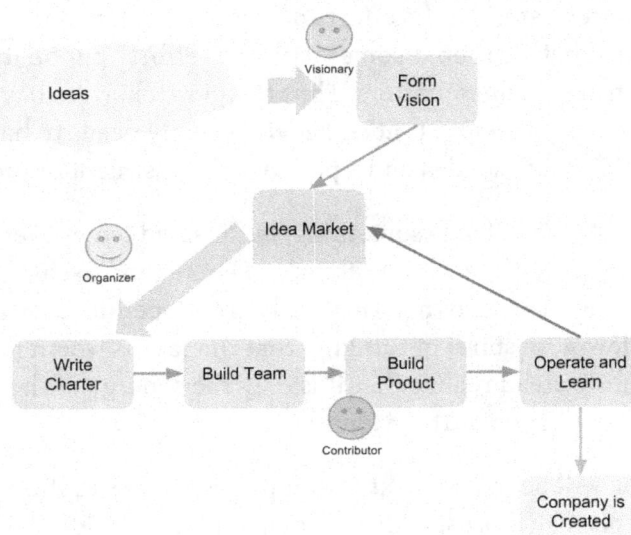

The idea market is the answer to the problem of finding a co-founder. It is possible that the person who was the Visionary to the idea handed the idea off to an Organizer to take it from there. By separating these talents out it allows for people to specialize. Ultimately it allows a person to be both the Visionary and the Organizer but does not require it.

So how does this work? The visionaries work on their idea until it is in a state that they deem presentable. At this point they submit the vision to this marketplace. Organizers looking for a project are able to see these visions and then write charters based on them. A notable side effect: If the idea is not well thought out and the effort put into it seems unreasonable then no one will want to implement it.

You might ask, "wait a moment, this is a market; what is being traded?". This is where things get interesting. The vision document should describe how much effort the Visionary put into this idea; this is essentially the "ask". An Organizer would be looking through these visions and trying to figure out how he would negotiate ownership of this Charter based on the efforts of this vision. Also if the idea has been tried before then it comes with the "effort" put on it by earlier attempts with other charters. Thus the more charters have been tied to the vision, the more is at stake. What really needs to happen here is a criticism of the idea and a possible readjustment of the effort.

The point isn't to trade something, but instead to get everything on the table in terms of what is at stake. People tend to think that their ideas are worth more than they truly are. Hopefully they are not going down the spiral of thinking that the idea is worth millions by itself, but instead realize that it is only the synergy of the idea and the team that will give it that value.

The idea will be judged next to competing visions in this idea marketplace. If a prospective participant likes the idea but thinks its stated value is incorrect, he or she can negotiate or walk away. There are two very important requirements here, and I want to emphasize them again:

1) The Visionary must figure out what the vision was worth to them and write it down.

2) The Organizer must judge the Visionary's assessment and decide whether to proceed.

People need to have a conversation very early about a tough topic: What is this worth to you? There is a lot of emotion tied up in this. Who knows what the inspiration was for the idea or what someone lost to come up with this vision? But in the marketplace of ideas, this conversation gets out of the way very early on instead of later when you are figuring out ownership.

On a human level, implementing someone else's vision is a very personal experience. The only way that co-founders at this level will understand this is to try and negotiate around this point. You simply do not know who a person is until you either marry them or try and start a business with them. Suddenly you find out about things that are important to them that make almost no sense to you. That's just life. We tend to hide how strong we feel about things because we want to keep things moving and avoid conflict. But in business, getting this conversation into the open at the founding of this relationship is vital, and the idea market is the tool that makes this happen.

The Charter Market

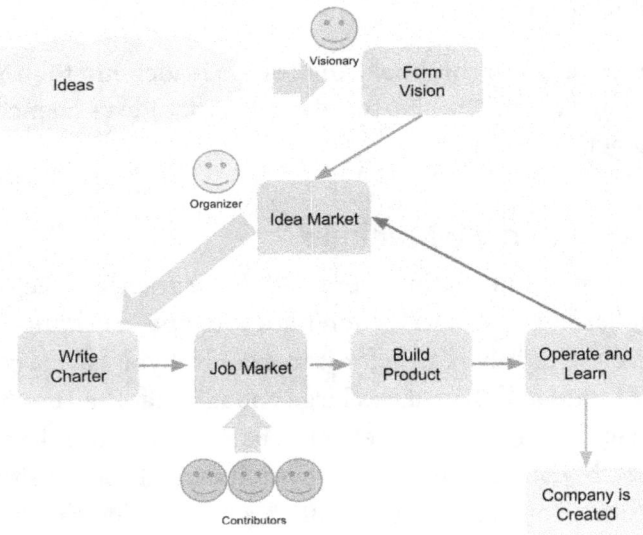

Here is a market for all other kinds of team members. Do you remember all those job requests that were created on the Charter? Someone has to fill them. I envision the charter market to be just this sort of place.

Every member of a team has constraints they have to stay within. This needs to be respected if you are going to build a real team and not just a bunch of people testing the situation. People need to know things like when the project will start, the required level(s) of commitment, what tools will be used, etc. If the vision and charter were created correctly then all of these questions will be answered by reading it. If not, then they should ask questions and help grow the charter further.

Members should be able to look for jobs they want to do within a set of parameters they specify. Maybe something doesn't come up. They can certainly go look for a vision in the idea market and build their own charter around it.

As stated earlier in this book, an idea is a leadership tool. You use it to gather your team. The charter market is that idea's chance to pull the team together.

Where are these Markets?

I want to point out that neither the "Idea Market" or the "Job Market" exist yet. At least, I don't know of one operating effectively.The only reason for it to exist is if you have a community of Visionaries and Organizers large enough that they don't already know each other. This market could be nothing more than a bulletin board with Visions pinned to it. It could easily be a website or in some other form. However, I don't think it is a technological challenge that prevents it from forming; it is the social challenge of trust. The market I described here requires the Visionary to put all of his work out for an unknown party to view. The fear would be that someone would simply steal the idea and work that went into it without giving the Visionary any sort of compensation for the effort he puts into it.

The same goes for the "Job Market". This is even more ripe for theft. In this case you have a preplanned recipe for building a company defined down to the set of tasks that need to be done. The only thing stopping your charter from spawning competition would be apathy.

For either of these markets to form and be used, more trust will need to be in place than a simple login or an NDA. It is my belief that first a society would need to form around this very set of activities. Something that speaks more toward loyalty and honor where being ostracized would be the punishment for not following the code I'm talking about.

If these ideas find a wide following I would consider building a society to create the trust needed to bring about usage of these markets. The websites would follow next as a fairly trivial web development project.

Conclusion

In following this process with these concepts a group of people can divide up the different type of work based on their interests and talents. They also have specific deliverables and expectations set at each point within the process.

What is key to note here is that one idea can spin off many Charters. These could actually be happening in parallel, or they could be spread out over decades. There is no reason for the lessons learned to be lost after the Charter is considered complete. It is also key to note that the pivots do not have to happen immediately. If the company completes a product, people do not have to just soldier on and keep changing direction until they run out of patience with the idea.

What this allows for is for the vision to be picked up by a completely different Organizer if necessary. As multiple Charters form from one vision, each might approach it from different directions; but the one consistent thread throughout the entire experience is the vision itself, and in the center of that vision, the initial idea.

Chapter 9: Including Investment

In creating ventures, actual money is involved at every point. It may just be the coffee and computers that are used to get something created and thought through. It may be for a space to work out of or to improve the image of the product. But, at every point a trade is happening. That trade is always executed in the spirit of doing something now in the hopes of gaining something better in the future. Farmers invest every year in their crops; workers invest every year in their companies; parents invest in our children. Investing in a venture, however, is different. It is building something that is so high-risk that you could easily never see *any* result from it.

Anyone associated with the venture is really an investor. It is just that the folks that had the idea and built it with no money are the most naive investors. As a software developer I had originally thought my role was to craft the product that was being sold. That certainly was true, but when there is no money involved then I am investing in the idea and in a pretty heavy way. My time may seem to have been worth little when I was in my twenties, but as I got older the value of one hour of my time increased. With a family to take care of, suddenly I needed to take my time and what I used it for much more seriously. When I was trading on just my own future, I was willing to sacrifice heavily, but when I was trading on my kids' futures in the process, the game was quite a bit different.

Investment groups were optimized to maximize investment for return. They want that one-out-of-ten explosive company that gives them a 50X return. They have clients themselves who have put money into a fund and they need to show that as a firm they can deliver. These clients want the next Google and the pressure is enormous. In this respect I think that anyone working on a startup needs to think about it from the investor's perspective: the investor needs that hit, needs it fast, and needs to spend as little money as possible on it.

I have heard that an investment rule of thumb is that one out of ten of your investments will be a hit, three others will go belly-up pretty quickly, three will be decent businesses, and the remaining three are what is called "the living dead." These last three drift on and on never really growing well, but never die.

The VC firm is really just looking that one-out-of-ten hit. But, from the perspective of someone *building* a company, a nicely growing business sounds great! I want that company that I can put my effort into that then pays dividends for a long time.

This seems to be a fairly obvious miscommunication. As a founder and investor my goals are very different from those of a VC firm. Sure, both of us are interested in making the trade of today's risk for tomorrow's rewards. But for me, I am happy with a lot less return than what they would accept.

Now, VCs represent one extreme. They are willing to put lots of money on an idea and lose it all. Banks represent the other extreme. They are willing to put a qualified amount of money on a business that will have a realistic return based on other businesses in its class. So the risk and reward sliders are different. Many angel investors want both worlds; they want the security of not losing their money, but they would like to be in on the 50X explosive growth.

My point is this: People and groups invest differently with different expectations, and you should understand their perspectives when you enter a deal with them. Your team most certainly should be aligned with the goals of your venture. Are you building a massively scaling explosive "startup" or are you building a solid "business"? Because even though "risk" and "reward" is what everyone talks about, the goal line might not be the same.

Up to this point, we've ignored the role of an outside investor in the processes outlined in this book. Now we'll touch a bit on what's involved for that role.

Incubation Process Revisited

Lets start by revisiting that previous process and I will show you where there are two points that investors will be able to influence. In one case the investor is approached by the organizer, in the other the investor approaches the organizer.

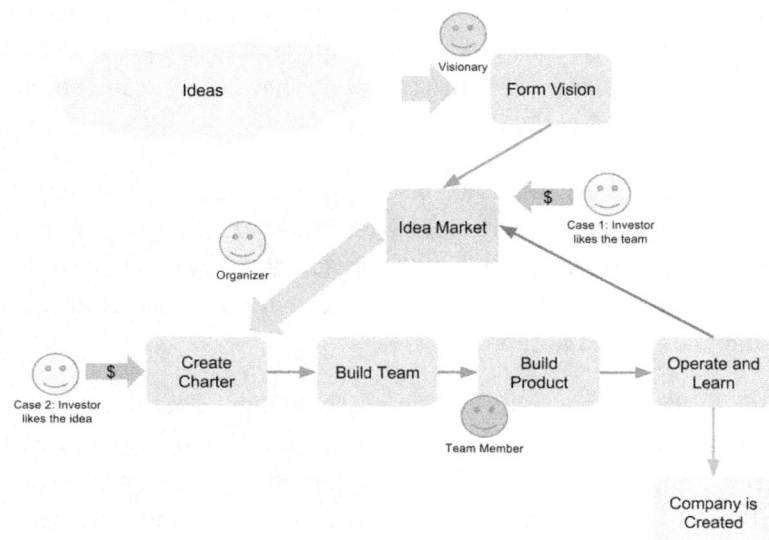

Case 1: An investor likes the team

In this case, the investor is willing to pledge a certain dollar amount, but they don't know which idea they want to put it on. This investor just knows that this group of people is one that she can trust, and is one she thinks will produce something.

What *should* happen is this: The dollar amount pledged is recorded and known. Then any organizer putting together a Charter should feel free to approach this investor to pitch the idea. If it looks like a match, then someone should define how this money will be used. At that point, you start to enter the types of conversations that are well documented outside of this book. For example, it will probably involve filing the company early on and establishing the relationship between the investor and the team that is being built around this idea.

Case 2: An investor likes the idea

In this case the idea is what has drawn the interest of the investor. In such a case, the investor approaches the leader with the intention of pledging money toward the idea. The conversation of negotiation happens afterward.

Investment Dollars vs. Recorded Dollars

One question that will come up is how the money gets used throughout the project. In the chapter about "accounting for effort", I brought up that everyone should have an hourly rate and be tracking this on a monthly basis. The purpose was to establish a baseline of effort so that team members don't find themselves in situations where one person is putting more effort into the idea than they are being rewarded for.

What happens, however, when an investor is involved? Do all of those numbers from budgeting and tracking effort translate directly to the real money that an investor is contributing? I think that the answer could be no or yes depending on the team.

From the team's perspective that number needs to be consistent. But the dollar amount invested are not necessarily dollars that the team are working from at that moment. The dollars invested may be tied to a discount on some agreed-upon 'standard' rate. For example, if an investor put down $10,000 for 100 hours then a discount rate of 50% was part of the deal. The investor has actually bought 200 hours of work.

Don't forget that the investor will want to see something tangible. So you will need to file the company by this point in order to provide the investor with shares. After that point you will be able to provide some sort of valuation for at least what you consider the worth of your business. For example, if you sell 100 shares to the investor and you retain 1000 shared, then the investor owns 10% of your company.

The whole deal would look like you traded 10% of the shares at $100 per share with a discount of 50% so that you would have 200 hours to work with. I don't know if that is a good or bad deal for your company, but at least it should be an understandable one.

Figure out when to look for help

It is assumed that you can get an idea together and rally a team around it. It is also assumed that everyone is excited about the project and starts working along.

You should also have created a time estimate in your Charter, as well as historical evidence of how many hours it took to get to where you are now. This is a great start and very important for justifying what you need to get to your desired goal.

There will be a point in the project when you are ready to involve an investor. It probably won't be at the beginning. Most likely it will be when you have created a minimum viable product (MVP) that you are seeing some sort of response to. Suddenly it is important to focus on it even more and scale it. This is when you will need help.

You should plan for this point ahead of time. You know when what you are building has reached a state where you can sell it, so why not contact people early? If you are new to this, you might want to give yourself at least three months. Use that time to network and to find people in the investment space. Make friends and explain what you are doing and when you might need help. You should be able to tell if what you are doing excites other people. That way, when it does come time to ask for help, you are not struggling to find people who might be interested.

Trust is everything

Remember that everyone must trust each other for this to work. Having proper legal documents is a must, but establishing the trust that you will do what you say you will do is essential. If you have been documenting your work from the vision all the way through the charter, then you will be able to build this trust. It shows that you have been able to plan and to execute on that plan.

It is also important for the team to see this behavior in action. Then they know that if you say something will take three weeks of their time and they will need to work hard, they can plan for it.

Most importantly, planning in this way builds trust in yourself. You will get some things wrong at first, but now you will be able to adapt and learn from your mistakes early. When you do talk to someone about investing in your idea, you will know where you came from, where you are going, and have the confidence to explain those to your would-be investor.

Chapter 10: Putting it all together

Blueprint of an Incubator

What we have examined in these pages thus far is how to take a group of people, collectively build up ideas, refine them, and turn them into companies. Along the way we have discussed everything from how ideas originate to the roles involved in the production of a product.

We also have spent a fair amount of time discussing the human commitments involved in building an actual startup and committing time into it.Retracing our steps through the chapters, we end up with a picture that looks like this:

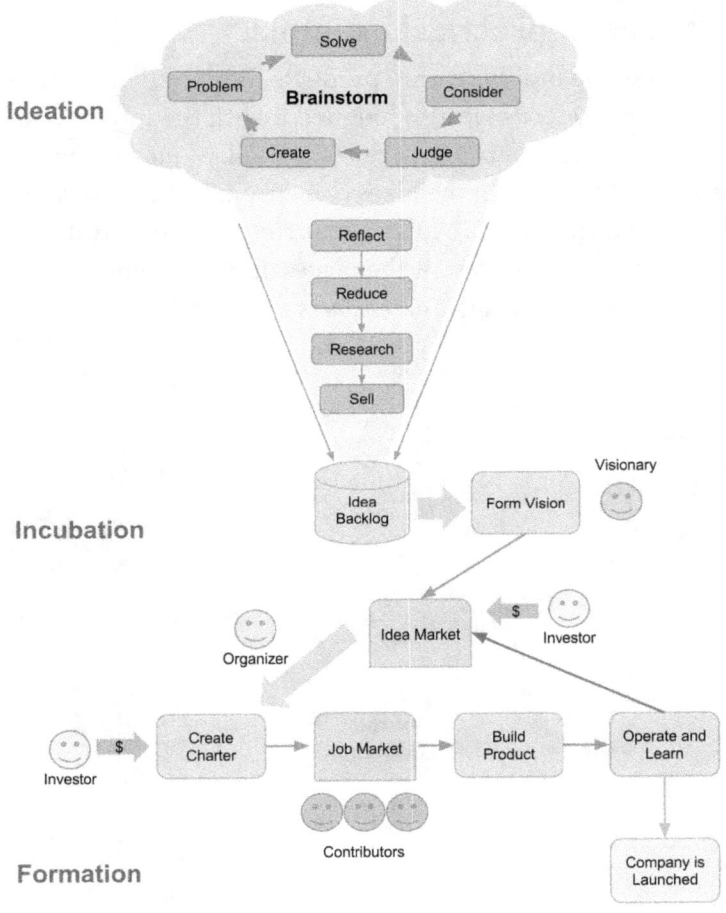

It's interesting to note that this process starts out as an idea living quietly inside someone's head and ends up over time as an enterprise involving other people. The top half of this drawing represents phases that could take place entirely inside your head. It isn't until you start reviewing the Vision with someone else that things get more 'extroverted.' This 'introversion' is nonetheless a huge and important step. As you move down through the drawing the process gets progressively more social. Once the idea is accepted and turned into a Charter, the team grows rapidly.

PugetWorks: A practical example

At PugetWorks, we build software products for our clients. Although this is our primary focus we also founded it with the intention of building our own products and services as well. A question we often wrestle with is "where will the ideas come from?" Our philosophy regarding this question has evolved over time; we've identified three 'idea tracks' that best represent the places our ideas tend to originate: *fun ideas*, *technology mashups*, and *business partnerships*.

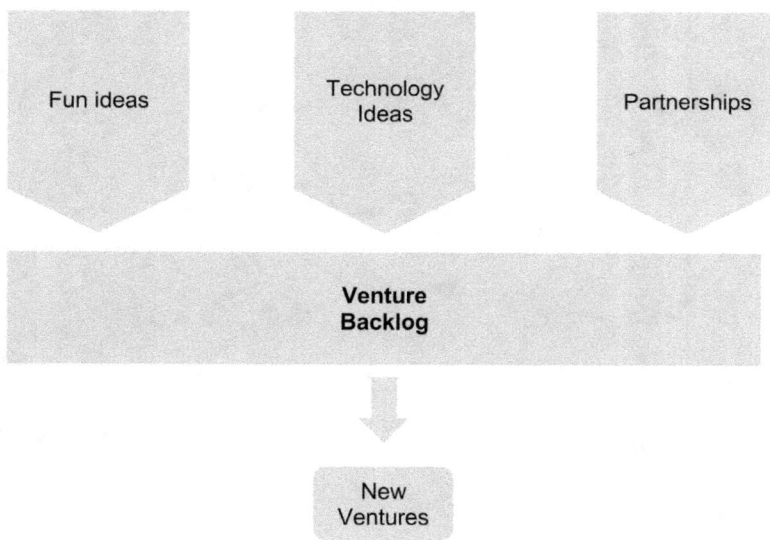

One thing to note is that the sources of ideas for us mapped to our personalities and to our industry. So this diagram might work if you are a software consulting firm, but it doesn't necessarily work for everyone. To explain a little further, let me explain each of our idea sources.

Fun Ideas

One friend of mine pointed out that software can be organized into the following loose categories: candy, vitamins, medicine, and heart meds. Candy is the fun stuff that you buy for recreation. You expect higher volume and lower margins. As you get to medicines, you are creating low volume / high margin software. Heart meds are the software products that industries can't live without. When I talk about "fun ideas," I'm of course speaking about the 'candy software' of the world, that goofy app that everyone has to download. It could be a tool, an amusement, or just some inside joke that might go viral.

An important subcategory of this is games. Everyone on our team grew up playing games and designing games. It is a source of fascination for the team at large. So we are naturally attracted to them. It's also important to point out that games are art. They don't really have any competitor except disinterest. Owning one game doesn't preclude you from owning another. So you don't have to worry about competing, only quality. If the game is fun, people will play it. This makes for a very fun set of ideas that we are still trying to figure out how to monetize.

The end result is that we are always coming up with game ideas. For that reason we keep a separate section simply for this.

Technology Mashups

When working on a client's software, you encounter some pretty daunting challenges - everything from processing millions of records an hour to building a model of the world in the cloud. We routinely have to work with images, videos, and GPS data, and we get involved in just about every industry.

What results is a very large code base that we maintain for different clients. In most of these cases, the code is owned by the client, but the ideas and knowledge we used to get there is our own. Essentially, if we did it once we can do it again.

So one source of ideas is that we can use this knowledge to rapidly construct prototypes. These prototypes can be built in a matter of hours, so it doesn't really need to be justified in the same way you would plan out a real product. Occasionally, something really cool comes from this process. Most of the time, though, it is just comedy and gets us thinking about the idea deeper. There has always been the possibility that with a hackathon we could come up with something really useful.

Partnerships

Finally, there are our clients and the entrepreneur community. As a consulting firm you get to know your clients very well. You get to know their dreams and ambitions. If you do this long enough you can spot flaws in their operations fairly quickly. Sometimes we can solve these problems or we can advise or improve their product. Because of this we get involved in some of these businesses in ways that are not easily explained.

I will tell you this: a bunch of engineers making mashups and dreaming up game ideas can't hold a candle to partnering with other entrepreneurs. When left to our own devices it is easy to come up with amusing products that no one really wants. They are really just diversions. What seems to holds us back is an understanding about an industry that only a business partner would have. It is when we find that passionate individual who is hell-bent on solving a problem that we find ourselves jumping in. These are our strongest ventures.

PugetWorks Venture Process

These three sources of ideas turn into visions and we work on them. Eventually we get to the point where we have the opportunity to really act on one of our opportunities. There are a multitude of possible reasons this can happen. Sometimes it's just that we ran out of other things to do; other times maybe someone wanted to invest into one of these projects.

If we expand the 'idea sources' model and apply the way we do design and creation, we end up with the following diagram:

Putting it all together

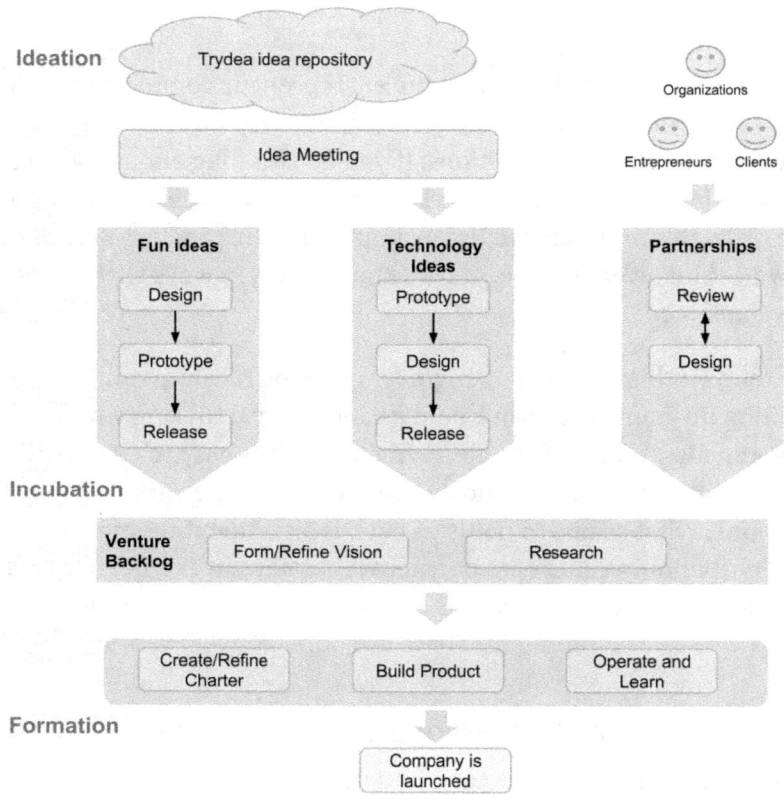

Parts of this diagram deserve some explanation. First off, ideas are coming in through a software platform called Trydea that I use to capture ideas using mobile devices and the web. You can find it on Github if you want to set up your own copy. It has a couple of associated mobile apps to help you capture your ideas offline.

From there, we try to get together to talk about these ideas, and the ones that start to make sense turn into vision documents. We do this work using Google Docs simply because it is so easy to create a new document and share it with everyone. Ideas grows naturally using this process. For a given vision document, people add competing ideas or new data, and we refine the vision over and over until what comes out of it is the strongest possible expression of the original idea.

Each track works a little differently. For a fun idea, it usually starts with some sort of graphical design, either wireframing or artistic compositions so that the rest of the group can understand how it will work. We would then build a prototype of it and release it. For technology ideas, we would first wire the parts together, then make it more usable by refining the design. In both of those cases we are trying to build something and get it out the door quickly so that we can see what the reactions are to the idea. Once launched, we can work on more of the vision driving the product.

The third track is for ideas that we encounter outside of our own domain of knowledge. This is what we have reserved for partnerships such as entrepreneurs, our current clients, or outside organizations. In this case we are not trying to build something to help refine the vision, but instead we are trying to capture the vision with a design. Usually this turns into a series of wireframes and screen designs as we carefully tease out details about the product from our partner. The end result defines what we speculate needs to be built.

All three tracks end up with a well-thought-out vision document in the venture backlog. From there we research and think about these different opportunities. If one of them is getting traction with the team or the outside world then we form our charter document to document how much risk and reward all parties would have on bringing the product to life.

It should be noted that since we are small, it is vital that we budget and limit how much time we spend doing any of these activities. Usually we are talking about 20 - 50 hours of effort to get a vision into the vision backlog. To budget for the charter we really have to look at what is needed to build the product and what the upside will be. All of these visions are competing with each other as well as our core business and this ends up causing quite a bit of debate.

One profound bit of insight I will leave you with is this: our size gives us an advantage in this process. We are a small firm of 15 people.

Since we have very concrete limits as to how much money can move through our organization, we must be cautious about what we are using our time on. This forces us to constantly evaluate the ideas we can manage. It also means we are constantly confronted with ideas that are simply too big for us to build or too risky to even start.

What about you?

Somewhere you fit into these diagrams. You probably have friends who can provide different perspectives. In the end, all you are doing is taking ideas, thinking them through, and deciding if you want to act on them. Now you have a blueprint for how to actually grow these ideas; the choice is yours.

At least, you can take this process and these templates and apply them to your particular situation. You don't have to do things exactly the same way we have. This should provide you with the tools that will make it easier to pull these ideas together and identify the ones you really want to pursue.

Formation

This section is devoted to advice for turning these incubated ventures into successful companies.

Chapter 11: Accounting for Effort

Before I started my first business, I remember never really talking about money with anyone. We all knew we made money and spent money. But it was somehow rude or uncomfortable to discuss the subject. After I started a company, however, that seemed like all we ever talked about. In fact, I started joking that the definition of a business was a series of awkward conversations with your friends about money.

Now that I have been doing this for a while it seems natural to think on this level. I'm a little surprised that our manners have grown to hide so much of what influences our behavior. At least in the culture I grew up in we didn't really talk much about money and I think this leaves us woefully unprepared for dealing with the world after it expects us to trade with it. As it is, a company is all about money. So you had better get used to it, and if you usually maintain a skill set that is insulated from money you will need to get in the mindset of everyone else who does.

Money means lots of different things in different contexts. It represents resources; it represents power, fairness, hopes, profit, and all sorts of things to all sorts of people. Some tie it to emotions or logic. Some use it to gauge success. For that very reason it needs to be integrated into a venture from the beginning.

It is possible to not talk about this subject and to just go out and build something. But I think doing so is taking an unnecessary risk. All you are doing is avoiding those uncomfortable conversations with your friends. If you are lucky enough for your company to matter, then you will have to have these conversations at some point anyway. It's best to do this early and get everyone on the same page before you find out someone has expectations that are vastly different from the rest of the group.

For that reason, this chapter is devoted entirely to how money is integrated into this system and some concepts and tools to help you set the expectations of the team from the beginning.

How do we calculate the value of the idea?

The value of the idea is a hypothetical number that doesn't upset the Visionary who conceived it, yet isn't so large that no one wants to work on it. It's a balance somewhere in the middle.

If you go back to the way a vision is calculated (Chapter 7) you will notice that the first section is a place to calculate the amount of effort. That is one of the hardest sections to fill out. What is being asked for is for the Visionary to explain how much this idea is worth to them. When we ask this question we are not asking Visionaries to guess the value of their ideas to the rest of the world. We need to know how much of *themselves* are in this idea.

"Why?" you might ask. There are two very important reasons: The first is we need a Visionary to specify what he or she has contributed to the idea thus far so that everyone else can judge if they want to work on it. The second and more important reason is so that the Visionary can come to terms with his own expectations toward that idea.

This idea might be a Visionary's 'baby'. This might be the best idea he has ever had. He may never see another idea like this one. But he also might not have the skills to produce it. The Visionary needs to get this down on paper and figure this out for himself or he can never really walk away from the idea.

By forcing someone to put a quantitative value on his idea we are forcing him to specify a place where he ends and the rest of the work begins. This is a very important boundary. If this boundary is never defined concretely, the Visionary will always feel slighted. He may feel like he was taken advantage of or that the original idea was diluted beyond his control.

I stated earlier that this might be the Visionary's best idea. He has recognized that he cannot do it alone, and now it comes down either to holding onto the idea and killing it, or handing it off and risking being used. These are two competing fears, and for a Visionary to really come to terms with his talents he must confront this head-on. You see, I don't think this truly will be the Visionary's best idea. I think this will just be his opening act, and the more he practices this art the better he will become. But he must take that first step and let it go.

Calculating an actual number representing the value of the idea helps the Visionary 'pass the baton' to someone else who will help take it across the finish line.

So how does the Visionary calculate the value of his idea? Strangely, he just picks a number and asks himself if it feels right. He writes this number down and asks himself, "Would someone want to join me if they knew how much I valued this idea?" If not, he'll need to lower it.

For the rest of us, I think we should all remember that this number is negotiable and we need to take the time to talk to the Visionary about this number and how he arrived at that value. A good analogy is someone trying to sell a house with an unrealistic expectation of its value due to emotional attachment. In the end, the house (and the idea) is only as valuable as the price a prospective buyer is willing to pay for it.

How do you budget creating a product?

Let's be completely honest on this part. It is total guessing and the quality of your guess will be related to how much experience you have doing this. If you happen to have had the pleasure of doing planning work for an organization, you will be better at this than someone who is just starting out. But it will come down to an understanding of how much work is involved, a process for completing this work, and a complete guess as to how fast each person can complete tasks for finishing the work.

Part of my life has been spent coming up with estimates for software projects, so I have a bit of experience doing this sort of thing, and there are several ways to go about it. Below I've listed a couple of tips. Just remember that this probably is the part that lots of people know how to do. So I'm not going to go into this in a whole lot of detail. There are many good books on estimating and running projects.

Divide the project into a building phase and an operating phase

The building phase is when creation is the most important activity. The operating phase is when selling is the most important activity. These could be happening in tandem; at every point in time you can pretty easily identify which is more critical at this moment. Sometimes you can't sell anything because there is nothing to sell. Sometimes you are building simply to help tune the product or service to increase its attractiveness. It is important to plan out when you will be in each of these phases.

It's also important to note that the team *building* the project is not necessarily the same team that will be *operating* it. These are two very different groups of people. You will probably have people involved in both phases, but the significance of their role changes. Your lead builder will probably fall into a support role. Your advisors in the building phase will end up selling the system in the operating phase. For this reason plan for two teams. One for putting it together and one for running it.

Plan everything as a series of sprints

If you are not familiar with Agile project management, I recommend for you to read up on this. You'll want to create a backlog of tasks and define how long you expect each sprint to last. A *sprint* is a period of focus for the team in which they will try to accomplish as many prioritized tasks as possible. It is assumed that the difficulties of tasks, their priorities, and the number of tasks are unknown at the beginning of the sprint but will be reviewed regularly to adjust expectations.

Yes, software development has reached the ultimate in project management flexibility. We can get away with this because the most expensive component is a worker's time, not physical materials. For other types of projects this might be different and you can resort to more standard ways of doing project management.

After you have set the sprint length and figured out the number of sprints you are going to have, it comes down to just estimating hours. You then assume each member can contribute 40 hours per week and multiply by that number. This gives you a rough picture of what's ahead.

Plan for a design phase

Here is a diagram I use a lot with software consulting:

Formation

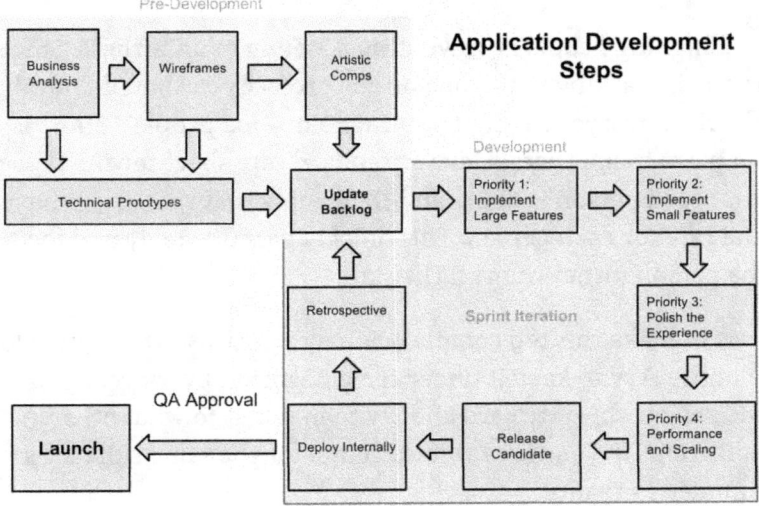

Notice that there is this bunch of tasks in the upper left that all lead to the backlog? This is the design phase. Make sure you allow time for these activities and have a good designer to work with to get through this. When you get to the part where people are making things, they will have much more direction if you have some picture of what they are suppose to build.

Tracking Members' Contributions

Time is money. You learn this when you do anything at an hourly rate, and I think that it helps when you look at the world this way. What is so wonderfully universal about time is that everyone is limited by it. I see time as being a less subjective unit of measure than money, and this is why I advocate measuring all effort on a project in terms of time rather than of dollar values.

So I recommend for each person contributing to the project to track his or her hours. There are a wide variety of hour-tracking tools out there, so this is a fairly easy practice to get into.

Assign Hourly Rates

Part of aligning people is preventing a feeling of unfairness. Since everyone is tracking their time on the project you should know how much effort everyone is contributing. But some people's effort is worth more than others. Make a standard rate sheet for the type of job that each person is doing and then apply that rate. Don't have a special rate for each person. This quickly gets unwieldy and focuses on the person rather than on the skill.

Try not to make this too complex. Some rate cards can get very long and clumsy. Try to keep it under ten categories. Every year you should review this rate card and try to match it to what other organizations in your area would charge for the same skill. This keeps it grounded in reality.

Also, make sure you make this rate sheet public. Everyone should have a chance to converse about how much their time is worth. Getting people on board early is key to prevent a general feeling of unfairness.

What happens to all this debt?

With these hourly rates and the team tracking hours, you start to see how time is being used and what could be accomplished when using real money. What you are seeing is the debt the project is accumulating. Hopefully this will track accurately against what you budgeted in your charter.

The philosophy here is to track everyone's contribution regardless of the situation. What should form is some sort of spreadsheet showing how much everyone has contributed over time. But now you have everyone looking at their individual debt put on a project. What happens?

The debt really is a tool for creating conversations early. So instead of that big frustration of "Bob owns 50% of this company and hasn't worked on it at all," you just have a weekly realization where it is pretty obvious the rest of the team is contributing and Bob isn't. This creates a social situation where this conversation is going to come up and whoever is organizing should address this far in advance.

Is this debt real money?

The debt is a measure of opportunity lost, cast in a very rosy light. When you look back at what it took to build something, these numbers can certainly change your perspective. For example, $120/hour is what we bill at my firm for software development. This rate isn't unheard of in Seattle and it could be argued that we could charge more. If you argue that a normal workweek is 40 hours/week, then the burn rate would be $4800/week.

Consider this: If you could make that sort of money, why wouldn't you do that instead of a venture? The truth is that you probably won't be able to do 40 hours of billable work in a week, but more along the lines of 60%-80%, and you won't be ignoring how much effort it takes just to find the work and maintain your existence as a business. This is what I mean by "rosy light".

These numbers are significant and shouldn't be ignored. So this doesn't necessarily represent money you can ever collect, but it does represent real effort that could have been used differently.

How do you justify your rates?

If you track this debt for years you will notice that it represents quite a lot of money. What happens if real money suddenly gets involved? You will be in a situation where an investor will question the rates you've selected. My advice is to pick rates that are realistic for your industry and location for tracking the debt. Your charter should have been planned out with some sort of budget that you are using to explain why you are accumulating this debt. For example, maybe you are receiving 20% of the company for 2000 hours of work. So the debt is really just showing how those 2000 hours have been used over time.

When it comes to the question of mixing real money with this debt, you always have the option of using a discounted rate. For example, lets go back to that example of 2000 hours budgeted. Let's say you are pretty bad at estimation, and ultimately you spent 4000 hours over three years to build your startup with your team. Your take was supposed to be 20% of the company. The product is great, and an investor is looking to help you amplify it. However, there is this odd problem: According to your spreadsheet, you used 2000 hours more than you had intended. At this point you either need to adjust your percentage in the company, argue that you should be paid for the extra time, or simply accept that your rates are 50% less.

The real money is different than recorded debt in that you may not have had an opportunity to really lose. The investor does. At least you have numbers to help you realize where your time was used and how that fit into your charter, so you will probably find a way to rationalize it.

Does this debt get paid off?

We expect that all the other people involved in this venture also track their hours. It is the only way to be fair all the way around. Do we ever expect that debt to be paid off? That is based entirely on your situation and what feels right. I know that is an odd answer, but it really depends on your ability to estimate in the charter as well as guess at several factors you could not possibly control or understand until after you tried to create and sell a product.

For example, lets say that your charter budgeted 1000 hours for you and 1000 hours for your friend to build something over one year. Each of you should have 50% of the company. But, after one year you have used 2000 hours, and your friend has used 500 hours. So there clearly is some issue with the balance of how the work was split out. At this point you should really renegotiate or this will stress your friendship.

So, yes, this debt needs to be paid off somehow. That could mean you get more of the company, or that the company has a recorded debt to pay you back over time. Essentially you just ended up being more of an investor than you had bargained for.

However, let's go with the same example again and change the parameters. If after one year you have used 2000 hours and your friend has used 2000 hours, then it would seem that both of you used 1000 hours more than you intended. This doesn't mean that the company necessarily owes both of you 1000 hours of debt. It just means that you and your friend are bad at estimations. So it probably doesn't make any sense to record that the company has a debt against you.

The point is to build out these ideas, not to milk them as soon as any profit is made. Debt is a tool that should be used to fix the problem of working in a world of unknowns.

What about contributions that are not hourly?

It is very possible for people to contribute key efforts to the venture that cannot be tracked by hours. The following are ways for accounting for this.

Paying for relationships

Some people can bring connections to an industry that would have been very difficult to get any other way. But you can't judge it based on how many hours the introduction took. Instead, judge it by estimating how many hours it would take to get that same introduction. How many people would you have had to contact? How many hours of working in that field? Then come to an agreement with the person who introduced you.

For some people their relationships are their most valuable contribution. It should be judged that way because they are giving you a huge boost in the right direction.

Commission structures

Commissions are great for motivating people. Especially the right type of person. Mainly a sales type person who craves to see a proportionate reward for the work he did. You should have the experience of building at least one such relationship. What is important is to realize that they are being paid by the debt they are making to the company. It may make sense to wait until you have a product to sell before you establish this relationship. However, if you have one person doing sales early on, it might make sense to offer a revenue share over a period of time instead of ownership. This aligns the person to the sales in the company which creates a win-win situation for both parties.

Partnerships

It is possible that your venture can be accelerated by working with other companies already in the same space as you. Partnerships are tricky, though. It comes down to good negotiations and mutual respect. Since you are starting from a very early position, you don't really have any leverage. But if you can find the right partnership, treat it the same way you would anything else. Track the money involved in the partnership as debt to the company.

Money Starts Conversations

Ultimately what I am advocating is to treat this as if it were a real company from the start and to build a budget as well as define all the financial relationships early. Track this with the same accuracy and tools that you would use if real money were involved. Then, figure out your billing cycle and invoice your company every month. This is a real debt that everyone should be able to see.

Money is uncomfortable, but you can make that fact work to your advantage. It sets expectations accordingly. Most importantly you will be able to judge how much effort was put into the company so that if someone does invest, you know immediately what your team has already put into the company. In this way, you can tell a good deal from a bad one.

This money, although virtual, will have a different effect. It will set the expectations of the team and let everyone understand their part in it. It will create several small conversations and adjustments. Best of all, it will also prevent one giant realignment if you were to ignore all of these contributions so that your team will stay together even if they are successful.

Chapter 12: Ownership

More important than selling someone on an idea is to align them so that if one person in the team wins then all of the team win. If you somehow create a situation where it is in the best interest of one member not to help the group, then you will be creating tension. Maybe that person won't give into the temptation to be selfish, but someone will feel that the situation is unfair.

Disaffection often starts over someone's percentage ownership of the company. Co-founders divide up the company early on; everyone gets some share of the company, and then off they go. Even in the best of situations, with the best intentions, resentment over ownership can arise, even accidentally.

The rest of this chapter is devoted to the following question:

Given an idea and a team, what apportionment of ownership will maximize everyone's motivation to stay engaged with the idea?

What doesn't work

Here are a series of situations I have been in and how this didn't work.

Wrong: Don't tell anyone how much the others own.
This is a silly situation, but it is a matter of control. If you are invited to a project and someone wants you to commit more in exchange for some ownership. But, if you don't know how much anyone else is holding onto then you can't even judge if its unfair. So the entire time you are working on the project you keep wondering what the arrangements are. Sure you could ask the leader, but it get awkward. What I found is that I just stopped trusting the leader and all the other members. I went back to contributing the minimum and the leader continued to just cajole us with guilt to keep contributing. So

what really happens is this backfires and the team become demotivated even though they own shares. The lesson from this, make sure the ownership structure is transparent. Whatever you do, make sure everyone knows what the starting point is and how this is going to change. Sure it might be in a legal doc but, no one really understands those. They want to trust their leader so the sooner you come forward with this information the better. If not you are only creating issues that will destroy your team.

Wrong: Have a complex structure

Once I was invited to join a startup. It was a new project for an older team. That team had a prior project and for simplicity didn't want to start a new structure but, instead reuse the old one. They also had a previous product so they didn't want new people to join on. So they had a five person LLC with one product already and I was bringing five people with me. My five people decided to turn into an LLC as well and then there would be a 50/50 partnership around the new venture.

So what happened? Well, I needed more contributed from the designer who was part of the first LLC. He only owned 10% of that LLC so essentially 5% of the product. It was also a LLC so the structure isn't easily changed. Basically the structure was useless and he wasn't very motivated because it all felt somewhat unfair. I think the only thing that motivated him was through the guilt of knowing the team at large wouldn't be making any progress. Basically "You don't want to be the guy that kills it right?"

After a while guilt wears off and turns into resentment. People either fade out of the picture or get angry. All of this over a silly structure for people who have no money going between them. The lesson here. Do not over complicate things. If you insist on starting a new company for every venture then pick clear dates to review the progress and ownership. If you are tracking debt and keeping everyone's expectations clear then you won't run into this problem.

Wrong: Your pie is really 110% in size.

After a startup is underway some people will not contribute as much as you were hoping. It happens; it's called 'life'. Kids, disease, love, and all those other things that should take a higher priority suddenly do. If you are the leader, then you should be prepared for this. Certainly, one way to deal with the change is to find another person to fill that role.

How are you attracting people? Is it with shares? Did you create an options pool, and are you working from that? The problem you run into is that people may not contribute effort commensurate with their share. You can identify this problem pretty easily when you budget the project and track hours with agreed-upon on rates. If you aren't doing this, then it is left to how everyone "feels" about the venture to decide.

There are many ways to approach this problem. One way is to make all shares, even early ones, vest over a time period. I personally think this is a good solution if you have to get the C corporation together before you actually get underway, but I would avoid filing the company until you absolutely need to do so.

A different option is to write the ownership down somewhere visible, and then schedule meetings to review how much effort people are putting into it. By the time you get to filing the company, your team will have agreed on what is fair.

Wrong: Focusing on ownership

I think this is an easy mistake to make early on. But it is one of the biggest motivating factors. Here is where the question becomes, "If I work on your idea, how much will I get?". It seems like an innocuous question, but it really is dangerous. Many people will want their shares to be proportionate, maybe even a little bigger than the other guys, but not so much that it looks wrong. Others, however, may bring an ego to the table and demand twice that which everyone else has. Eventually we will all come to terms on some percentage.

The situation is essentially a negotiation, but one in which all the leverage is speculative. The person with the connections or idea has some leverage. The person building it also has the leverage that he can simply walk away at any time. But, this is a really terrible way to decide who gets the most of anything.

The most important point here is that it really doesn't matter unless everyone involved is successful and the company has an IPO or gets acquired. There is a third success case, one where the venture is doing well as a company and dividends are being distributed. But, I don't know many ventures that argue on these terms. Most people have fears that their rightful share will get diluted, that they'll get cheated. No one wants to look like a sucker. So everyone puts up a little fight.

You might as well be kids in a sandbox arguing over who is going to own what part of the world. It is important to make sure the other kid doesn't get all of the world, but if you are fighting each other then you clearly are not taking over the world. It's a moot argument.

Wrong: Too many owners

Diluting the ownership also dilutes the responsibility and that in turn lessens how committed everyone feels they need to be. You can have owners who are sort of lurking. They don't really contribute much, but they have a share.

If you just have two owners then it's pretty hard to hide from what you've committed to. On the other hand, If you have ten owners it gets pretty unwieldy. In my personal experience, I've found three to be the sweet spot for the number of owners of a venture. Three tends to promote good debate, as long as no one has a majority and uses it to bully the others. Everyone will keep talking as long as they have a need to convince the others.

What works well

Ultimately there are two things that people want to know: 1) whether everyone else in the group is matching their commitment; and, 2) what will happen if the venture succeeds. To address these concerns, I recommend the following:

Figure out the value contributed *before* you start

This is a tricky conversation, but one that is extremely important for the co-founders to have. If someone is contributing relationships, the idea, prototypes, domain knowledge, or anything else before the project starts, you need to record that value. The value is for that person to decide and for the others in the group to accept.

This is that section at the top of the Vision documents that is asking for "Efforts". This lets it be recorded that someone has contributed, and then it is just a debate around everyone's assessment of that contribution. Getting this figured out before you begin will help greatly, both in deciding if you want to involve this person, and if that person wants to be involved.

Track Debt

This was talked about in the previous chapter, but it is important enough to reiterate here. For the entire course of the project, you should track the time people are putting into the project. Do this with hours. The hour is the one immutable currency that we all hold in common. For that reason it is perfect for equalizing effort. Everything should be phrased in terms of hours. From that you can use an hourly rate to weight the types of efforts in the group. And from all of this you will need to put together a spreadsheet and update it monthly so that the others can know what is going on. Make sure this is available to everyone in the group so anyone can see the effort the others are putting into the project.

This is very good practice, because if you ever want to renegotiate ownership then everyone can see how much effort they all have put into the project.

Wait to file the company

Filing a company is about declaring the ownership to the government so you can be taxed appropriately. So you do need to do this before you can have money moving through your venture. Until you get to that point you can keep all of this limited to your spreadsheet. Yes, it is more legal to get it filed, but it is also more difficult to change anything. If you don't trust your business partners to respect what is agreed upon on paper then you probably shouldn't be starting a venture with them, anyway.

Plan to renegotiate

Set a couple of meetings in the future where the ownership conversation will be revisited. This lets everyone prepare to justify what they did and to get all of their complaints out in a compartmentalized way. It would make sense to revisit it after the MVP is built and after the venture has been operating for a couple of months. In that way, everyone knows how much effort was really contributed.

Vesting

Another way to avoid an imbalance of effort is to make everyone *vest*. This means that they have a set number of shares budgeted to them, but only based on performance. You can use this to dole out shares over a period of time. If you have to declare the shares early, then this shows everyone that those shares are contingent upon the project's success.

Option Pools

This is a pretty important concept. It allows you to set aside a percentage of the company to give to future recruits. In most cases it comes with a vesting period. Designing in something like this from the beginning provides you with some alternatives to making everyone a founder. Founders tend to have large percentages that get diluted as the company moves forward. If you've ever been involved in a startup, then chances are good that you were given shares from an options pool.

Don't forget about other ways to reward

Not everyone needs to be an owner to want to be involved. But, everyone does need some sort of incentive to take risk. A percentage of ownership is just one way to do this. Other tools at your disposal include revenue sharing, convertible debt, and sales commissions.

Revenue Sharing

This concept is fairly simple. Someone contributes to the project; in exchange they get a share of revenue for a period of time. You will need to negotiate the percentage, the duration (if that percent can change later on), and whether the money comes from gross or net revenue.

This works really well when you already have something and need to grow it (for example, if you already have an audience and need a new product). In such a case, you can work with someone to build that product in exchange for a portion of revenue. It is a bit tricker when everything is speculation, but you can reward them well for a shorter period of time. This strategy works really well when someone doesn't really want to commit to the company for the long term, but would like a medium-sized return on a period of sustained effort.

Convertible Debt

This is basically an IOU that can later be converted into shares in the enterprise. This becomes a debt that you must pay off at some later date. Things requiring negotiation include: when this will be paid off; what happens if you can't pay it off; how the debt will be converted; and whether interest should be applied.

Probably the biggest problem here is the date you pick for paying it off. If you don't know what your revenue is, then it is really hard to predict when this will become possible.

What this does solve is the problem of disagreeing on the value of the company. It allows you to resolve that disagreement essentially by agreeing to decide on it later. But if you can agree to a target value, it would be better to think in terms of shares early on. That way you are aligned from the start.

Sales Commissions
When it comes to doing sales you need to incentivize people to do this. You need to let them be rewarded when sales get filled. However, *don't* do this with shares. Look into commission structures and how to get your sales team organized. There is a good reason that this is its own section on the Charter.

When you do sell your product, you'll want to decide how much of that revenue should be budgeted toward the sales activity itself. That gives you a percentage to work with. Then it just comes down to how that percentage works and how long it will last.

You should also define your sales process. Commonly it is divided into lead generation and closing. But you can have account management, geography, or seasonal rules as well.

What you want is a well-defined way to reward people for selling the company in a way that is complementary to your business.

Ultimately, What is an Owner?

Ownership

Being an owner is about control. It is the control of being able to steer something that you are trying to build. Without it you will have to influence those who *do* decide. Ultimately, if you manage the business correctly, it will be about dividends or a payout from an IPO or acquisition. But this is so far down the road, it's almost comical.

Regardless, someone needs to own the company and you want those people to be the people who are going to sacrifice with you to make it happen. You don't have to agree with these people 100% of the time, but you will need to be able to make decisions together.

Chapter 13: Structural Recipes

This book was written over the course of several years. Even before it was written, we had tried different techniques and ways to distribute opportunity, risk, and ultimately, reward. The ultimate goal in this journey has been to make sure that everyone stays aligned - not just to make sure that we all stay happy, but also to ensure that our organization remains adaptable.

Originally when we started PugetWorks we wanted "to get ten smart people in a room every day". This ended up being fairly easy. First, you rent a room, then tell all your friends with contracting gigs to come sublet. Eventually, you find enough people to hang out with in that room.

One of the first things you discover, though, is that it is chaos: people showing up at random times, disturbing each other, eating strange food at their desks, and more. So we created lunch rooms, offices hours, and quiet times. From the ground up, we had to build a society that was dynamic, but effective.

The next thing we found was that not all of our friends had all the skills to thrive as the founders of a startup. So we started hiring them as employees and managing the stuff they were not good at so that they could focus on the things that they *were* good at.

Next, we found that other people liked those skills of our new employee-friends and wanted to recruit them for their projects without taking into account all of the overhead we were dealing with. So then rules had to be established to prevent this sort of odd unfairness.

Things progressed like this for a while; we would come up with solutions to one problem or another and then deal with new problems that arose afterward. This cycle created for us a society of experimentation, one where we were attempting through trial and error to balance fairness, effort, and passion. Below, I'll list some successful 'design patterns' that came out of our struggle.

Pattern 1: Big-Slice/Small-Slice Rules

This design pattern is concerned with the problem of how to allocate ownership dynamically and transparently. It solves this with a two-step process. First we budget percentages of shares for different phases. Then we dynamically allocate those shares by tracking the amount of work each team member does in that phase. I like to visualize the entire set of shares as a pie graph with each budgeted phase as a slice of that pie. The name of this comes from a friend who once told me "a big slice of a small pie is just as good as a small slice of a big pie". In this case, he was using the metaphor of a dessert pie, and this process is something like your team standing around figuring out who gets how much of what slice.

Step 1: Budget

Visualize all the ownership, shares, of your company like a huge pie. You need to decide what the different phases and activities are worth in terms of the whole endeavor. Normally this is just the number of shares created and percentages that each owner would have.

Formation

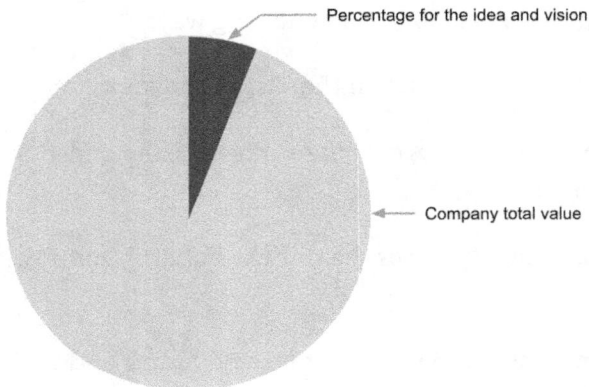

Start with the idea itself and the work put into the vision created for this idea. Is the idea worth 50% of this pie? Is it worth only 5%? Maybe it was 10%? It may help to look at how much effort was put into the idea in the vision document.

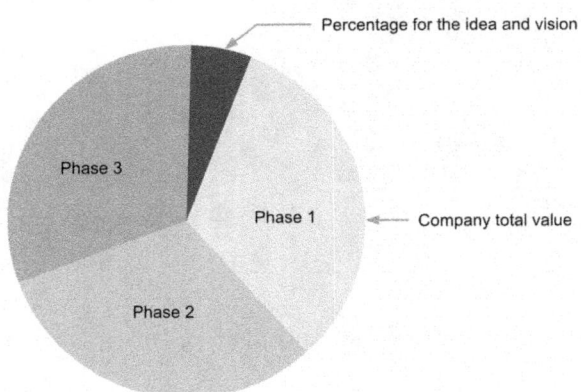

Next, imagine how many times you might need to pivot to make this idea a reality. Three is a pretty safe number. I have been calling these phases, each ending with a pivot. In each phase there is a period of building and then a period of operating the business.

The resulting pie is sliced up in the following way:

- 10%: for the work done on the Vision and idea.

- 30%: for Phase 1: 15% of that for the building and 15% for operating it.

- 30%: for Phase 2: 15% of that for the building and 15% for operating it.

- 30%: for Phase 3: 15% of that for the building and 15% for operating it.

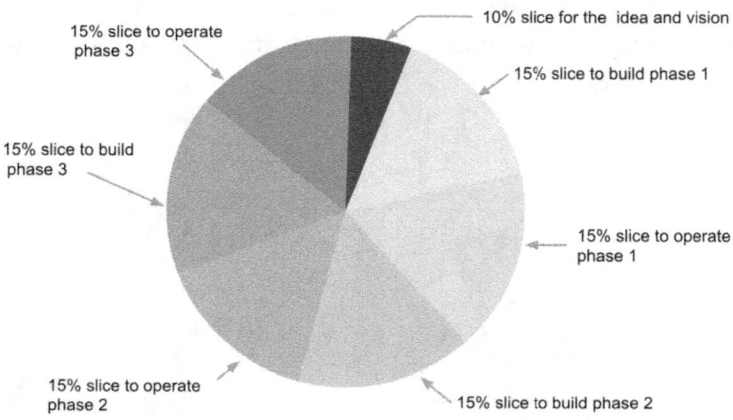

This gives you a pie that looks something like this:

Do note, that these numbers and phases could be very different for your organization. This is only a suggested way of dividing up the pie.

Step 2: Track effort in each "slice" and allocate it dynamically

This ties directly to Chapter 10, accounting for effort. In that chapter

I advocate keeping a weekly tally of how many hours each member has put into the project. You would then use this tally to figure out what percentage of the slice each member has. Do note that this percentage is limited to the slice they budgeted in step 1.

An example

Jim, Bob, and Mary want to build a company. First, they decide that the idea that Bob and Mary have been working on is worth 10% of the total pie. They then split the remaining into three phases, each with a budget for building and a budget for operating it. So the pie is split up exactly the way described above. Then they start tracking time as they build out the idea and the following story unfolds:

Idea and Vision: 10%

Mary did half of the work on the vision so she gets 50% of the 10% slice. This translates into 5% of the company. Bob did half of the work on the vision so he gets 50% of the 10% slice. This translates into 5% of the company.

Building Phase 1: 15 %

Week 1: Bob works 10 hours, Jim works 10 hours, Mary works 30 hours.

Week 2: Bob works 10 hours, Jim works 10 hours, Mary works 30 hours.

At this point the product has been built. Bob put in 20 hours, Jim put in 20 hours, and Mary put in 60 hours. So their percentages of this slice are as follows; Bob 20%, Jim 20%, Mary 60%.

Translating this into shares of the total company would be as follows:

- Bob: 20% of the 15% slice = 3% of the company.
- Jim: 20% of the 15% slice = 3% of the company.

- Mary: 60% of the 15% slice = 9% of the company.

If we were to tally how much each person has of the company to this point you would see this:

- Bob: 5% for the idea, 3% from phase 1 = 8% total.

- Jim: 0% for the idea, 3% from phase 1 = 3% total.

- Mary: 5% for the idea, 9% from phase 1 = 14% total.

Operating Phase 1: 15%

In this phase, Jim did most of the work of running the company as the group learned about their product and customers. So we see the following:

Week 1: Bob works 10 hours, Jim works 30 hours, Mary works 10 hours.

Week 2: Bob works 10 hours, Jim works 30 hours, Mary works 10 hours.

The tallies for this slice are; Bob 20 hours, Jim 60 hours, Mary 20 hours. This makes each member's percentage for the slice as follows: Bob 20%, Jim 60%, Mary 20%.

Translating this into shares of the total company would be as follows:

- Bob: 20% of the 15% slice = 3% of the company.

- Jim: 60% of the 15% slice = 9% of the company.

- Mary: 20% of the 15% slice = 3% of the company.

If we were to tally how much each person has of the company to this point you would see this:

- Bob: 5% for the idea, 3% from building phase 1, 3% from operating phase 1 = 11% total

- Jim: 0% for the idea, 3% from building phase 1, 9% from operating phase 1 = 3% total

- Mary: 5% for the idea, 9% from building phase 1, 3% from operating phase 1 = 17% total.

At this point, Bob, Jim and Mary realize they are building the wrong product and their customers really wanted something else. So they decide to pivot and change directions. They would start the whole process over again for phase 2. If Phase 2 turns out to be a success, they could always forgo doing Phase 3 and dissolve the percentages budgeted toward it into their own percentages.

Advantages

All of this is very easy to calculate and perfect to put into a spreadsheet. If you make sure the spreadsheet is public then everyone can see how their work is translating into shares of the company.

One of the greatest advantages here is that you can add and remove people dynamically. If you wanted to add someone new in Phase 2 you simply give them a column on the spreadsheet.

The end result is that as people file hours, their percentage increases. By the time you finally have a company up and running, you also have all the accounting of who did what to get there.

Problems

This is an easy way to get past the ownership talk. Everyone can fit into this structure in some form, and it allows people to be added and removed easily. At the least, it gets you to the point where something can get built.

However this structure does introduce some problems. This is what we learned:

You end up with a lot of owners
When you do go to file the company you now could have several owners who only put an hour into the whole project. This might create complications later since now this isn't a traditional startup with a small number of founders, but instead a collective of people.

This is solvable, but when the company is ready to be filed you will need to talk with all of your myriad contributors and make sure their efforts are being addressed correctly. Maybe options from the options pool make more sense in this case.

Not everyone's work has the same value
Some people may have skills that are more valuable and want their efforts to reflect that. This is easily solvable if you apply a rate to the hours they provide. This is exactly the same as an hourly rate being used with real money to adjust for value. You may want to refer to Chapter 10 on accounting for effort.

There may be no actual momentum
With a fluid management like this, you can easily have everyone contributing as they want to. For us, this sort of situation made it hard to build momentum, especially when team members have differing levels of motivation or inspiration toward the project. In such cases, we found it best to give a smaller number of people larger shares; this would motivate that small group to commit lots of effort for a short period of time (one year or less).

If your project just needs to get done, and get done fast, the idea of spreading ownership widely might not be the best approach for you. This approach works better for a two-year project where you might expect to course-correct several times.

There is a bit of administration
This approach does require your team to constantly track hours. This can be a bit tedious and can even cause a bit of stress for people. I

would argue that this is better than the alternative of not tracking anything and having one big conversation later.

Pattern 2: Convertible Debt + Revenue Share

Our friend Scott White founded the iPad application "Reading Raven" and used a bootstrapping methodology that allowed him to take his idea and turn it into a reality. We were involved in it at the beginning and really thought the process was an excellent one for taking a single idea and making it a reality.

Step 1: Use convertible debt for professional help.

At the very beginning Scott had found an idea that he was passionate about and proceeded to think it through on the side. At a certain point he realized he needed professional help with the user interface, but he did not have enough financing to use all of his money for that part. So, he offered to use a convertible note to cover the debt of working with a professional user interface designer. The convertible debt was essentially an IOU that could later be converted into shares or cash depending on how well the company performed.

Step 2: Use a seed pool of money to pay a developer

What Scott did have was enough cash built up to pay a developer to then create the prototype designed in Step 1. Depending on the developer and their situation he might have been able to use only convertible debt at this point. But, this would be only in the case that the developer could handle the risk.

It should be noted that by paying the developer, the developer was able to focus instead of treating Scott's project as a side project. This ultimately allowed it to get put together more efficiently.

Step 3: Use the prototype to recruit more people with the revenue share arrangements.

At this point Scott had a good working prototype, but it wasn't complete enough to sell. So he used his prototype to get others excited about his vision and to want to contribute. To compensate them, he worked out how they would be paid back based on the revenue generated by the product. It wasn't complex math, but it did require thinking about all the cost and how these recruits would get part of the gross profit for a period of time.

Step 4: Offer to convert the convertible debt into revenue share.

Just before launch Scott offered to turn the original convertible notes back into revenue share. At this point, everyone could see what the product is and speculate on how well it would do. If particular individuals wanted their money back sooner, they could take the revenue share.

Using this process Scott was able to pull together a product almost out of thin air. I have always thought this methodology would be very helpful for someone working a full time job, and with the right contacts they could organize the construction of a new venture.

Pattern 3: Benevolent Dictator

This pattern is actually one that *didn't* work out for us. I add it here for completeness and to show our progression over time.

Running a consulting business was hard, and we simply were overwhelmed with the work of pursuing projects and finding clients. In the process of handling all the business we found it difficult to consult the team on every business decision that needed to be made. So we stopped doing so.

A small group of us focused on drumming up new business, and between paying projects we came up with *new* projects based on what we thought the rest of the team might like to work on. We had the best of intentions, as they say; as it turns out, though, the team would have preferred to have some say in new work that would be tossed their way, interesting or not.

Our 'benevolent dictatorship' backfired; our team felt no ownership in the new ventures we initiated, and those new ventures came to be seen as a drag on the team rather than as cool new 'skunkworks' projects for the team to get excited about.

You're probably reading this and thinking to yourself, "What's the big deal? Every corporation in the world has executives and project planners who dictate what the people underneath them do every day, and this doesn't seem to cause them problems."

To that I say, yes, that has traditionally been true. In the industry we're in, individual empowerment is very important. You can see how larger technology companies try to empower their employees through different means, such as 'hack days', or '20% time' (in other words, time to pursue personal projects). These approaches may work well for them.

In the case of a tiny org such as the one we founded, however, the only way to have real empowerment was to give everyone say in what we did as an organization. We had no choice but to do the hard work of soliciting opinions, building consensus, and somehow coming out the other side with viable business goals.

Pattern 4: Venture Club

Part of the problem with the benevolent dictator pattern was that a small set of people owned everything and thus there was no way to really include the rest of the team in the decisions of what to build and how they would benefit. This core problem is where most incubators fall apart. The people who need to be invested in the idea simply do not have any real say.

To address the problem of ownership, we invented a new pattern: the 'Venture Club'. We realized that we had to find a way of giving everyone on the team a means of having some 'skin in the game.' Instead of making it one person's responsibility to find the perfect project, we distributed that responsibility across the whole team. It was required that every member of the club contribute monthly to the funds used by the club to finance ventures. Think of it like an investment club, but for a startup's projects. We shared ownership and risk; in this way it became more like a worker-owned cooperative. Here is how it would works:

Step 1: Form an LLC

File an LLC and then create a bank account. The LLC needs to have voting shares and ownership shares.

Step 2: Everyone contributes monthly

The money goes in the bank account and builds up. This is what can be used to invest in any other venture.

Step 3: Members propose and vote on ventures.

Each member can propose a venture with a charter. Then the voting members vote on if they want to invest the money into this venture. Realize that the money might be used to pay someone to quit their job, or it might be to hire a contractor, it could be used in any way that the charter describes.

Step 4: On success, the money goes back into the club

If one of the ventures is successful then the money goes back to the club. This can then be reused to power more ventures.

Step 5: Payout

Assuming the ventures pay off, then you simply do a distribution to the owners based on shares. This also makes a good solution to the group never finding anything to put their money into.

Problems

In our case it was questionable if this was even legally possible having our firm also organize this club. We had considered giving everyone a raise so they could invest in the club. With that came the risk that they might not, and our consulting company couldn't tell them they had to. So for the case of an existing company doing this, it wasn't really possible.

However, I think this design is superior if you have a group of people who want to build something and don't know what that is yet. This especially holds true if they are willing to try building *several* things to get there. Since they are first working on their visions and then charters to be reviewed, the businesses that come out of the effort would be stronger.

What if someone wants to have more ownership of a company they are proposing?
The answer is, that person puts this desire into the charter, and if the club believes it to be fair, then there is no problem. In a way this makes sense because someone will need to drive these businesses. Not everyone can be armchair entrepreneurs.

Incremental Proposals

Ultimately the Venture Club pattern would not work for my company because of our history and responsibilities. As an already-operating company we had plenty of time to work together; we could afford the resources that we needed to build a team that was very interested in innovating. But we also had responsibilities outside of the consulting firm. We were all having children, paying for houses, and had others who depended on us. So we had to master consulting first. We really didn't have a choice; we were coming from meager backgrounds, and the only other alternative would have been to take jobs and meet on the weekends. It became very apparent that the consulting model was the only model that would work for us.

Because of the way our business works, we could essentially do paid work half of the time and work on our own stuff the other half of the time. When organized properly this can be done well. I do want to stress that we were very efficient as a consulting firm, in my humble opinion. It's not something that happens overnight; it took us a good five years before things felt like they were getting easier. It's especially difficult during a down market.

This final pattern works the best when you have an already functioning company and want to bootstrap ideas internally. It is intended to be a pragmatic approach that doesn't disregard your core business while at the same time allows your team to explore other ideas so you may find a new direction.

Step 1: Experimentation (with Limits): Side Projects

The way this has worked out for us is that we created a program where anyone could propose a side project. This allows for our group to grow domain knowledge, products, and skills collectively. Every Side Project was tracked in a time-tracking system and limited to just 20 hours total. Most importantly the Side Project would result in a presentation to the group. This presentation could be a technology demonstration, a market that was researched, or just a concept that sounded really interesting.

To propose a side project the following had to be worked out ahead of time:

- Title

- Date to finish by

- Explanation of what it was

- Explanation of why the team member wanted to pursue it

The decision to do a side project was left to the individual, but we provided the following guidelines:

- It shouldn't duplicate what someone else has already done

- It should serve the group's benefit, not just that of the

individual

- It should be somewhat related to our core competencies

- If unsure about the idea's viability, a discussion should occur. Peer review always helps.

We scheduled a two-hour meeting to happen every other week on a Friday afternoon. If a project was done by then, an individual could present it to the group. What this did was create an outlet of discovery, where everyone could explore ideas and if their presentation inspired someone else, they could take it further.

From a management perspective, we looked at it like this: If five people each did two side projects per year, then we were looking at burning a maximum of 200 hours per year. The project provided an outlet for creativity and kept people imagining. The presentations helped explore ideas that we couldn't direct very easily.

So with this 200-hour budget per year, we formed a machine that could come up with Visions and continue to explore them. The side projects became a way to build up visions and to explore them as a group, but with well-understood limits.

Step 2: Allow Proposals to Come From Within

Some of the visions grew and became bigger than something that could be done in 20 hours. To get to the next step, a charter was needed. This charter had to describe the tradeoffs for a larger commitment from the company and from the individuals who work in it.

It had to be acknowledged that the company would be the investor at this stage and would take the biggest risk. This needed to be addressed first, either through the percentage of ownership or a revenue-sharing agreement. In any case, the charter needed to state this.

It also had to be acknowledged that the individual who was proposing this felt some sort of passion toward it. Maybe it was only enough that they wanted to build it; maybe it meant the world to them. This was addressed in the charter by what everyone else was going to get out of the deal. If that meant the person with the idea and proposal would get 5% as a finder's fee, or 50% because this was their passion, then that needed to be proposed. The trick here was to make sure people worked together to think through these charters. We would debate it ahead of time so that it was clear how much everyone would own if it worked.

The charters became a way to start the conversation and ended when we had a plan that everyone was comfortable with.

Step 3: Payout

The charter address this when the venture begins. It should state how much each group owns or whether there is some sort of revenue split. So that part is fairly well-specified. But what about the people who worked on the project on behalf of the company? I don't mean the people pitching the charter, but your friend who actually coded it?

In this case you have to do a profit-sharing model. Lots of articles exist on this subject so I won't explain it completely here. The general gist is that you want the actual profits from the venture to go to the people who contributed, but only after the business is working. So don't kill the new venture by pulling all the money out from it too early. The point is to grow this into a new company that will probably have its own employees and management.

Why not just give everyone a little of the company that was created? You could do it this way. You have to realize, though, that in making a long-term commitment to your employees to build something external to the company they currently work for, you have unintentionally aligned everyone in an adversarial way.

This is subtle and very important, so let me try to explain it further. Imagine that you own a company, and that you have an employee,

Bob. Bob works on your ventures, and you give him a little piece of each one. Then, he will hope that the ventures succeed so he can quit working for you. But, if you instead provide a profit-sharing program so that when the venture works out he gets some sort of boost, then he will *want* it to work out so that his current company continues to exist.

If you are considering allowing your company to create companies, you have to make sure that the people who work with you want those companies to succeed.

Results

This pattern resulted in some elaborate plans. Some involved convertible debt to get the project to a certain point. Others involved revenue sharing.

There are several key points to take away:

- Side projects allowed visions to grow internally

- Charters documented the proposed plan and got the conversation to happen between the individual and the company

- The commitment of a company was required to the individual

- The individual had to realize that the company was taking a risk on them

- The individual had to trust the company to follow through with these commitments and the company had to trust the individual to work with them.

Conclusion

Trust can only be created by working together. But without a *way* to work together, how do you form that trust? You can only do so by coming up with a plan and then following through with it. When things go bad, you have to talk through them. It's the right thing, even if it is hard.

These recipes provide a couple of different plans to help form this trust over time. Depending on the objective, different plans may prove necessary.

To summarize:

- **Big Slice Small Slice** should be used by groups that know what they want to build and want to limit commitment;

- **Convertible Debt + Revenue Share** is a great way to organize a project when you are the visionary and organizer;

- **Venture Club** should be used by groups that don't know what they want to build and are willing to put effort into it for a long time;

- **Incremental Proposals** should be used by existing businesses that want to spin up new things;

Oh yeah, and in my opinion no one should use the **Benevolent Dictator** pattern.

If you are designing this yourself and striking out in a new direction, remember that this is entirely about alignment. If your design does not align everyone to the same goal, then it will fail. So think about what people will value and how they will play out in your model. Review the design with those who actually will be doing it. If anyone can find a flaw in your logic, it's them.

Chapter 14: Company Formation

Forming a company is a big step. It involves the paperwork of telling the government that you exist, but more importantly it is a signal that you are ready to involve money. There is a lot of information around explaining the mechanics of what you should file as well as when it's best to do so. I'm not going to repeat the details of that process here.

This chapter pertains to explaining the team transitions when you are ready to file this company. The reason this is so important is that when you file your company, you are drawing a line in the sand. You are declaring who owns how much of what. If you have been following the process outlined in this book, it should be somewhat mechanical. Everyone on your team knows what is going to happen and how much they would own. However, there are still a couple of questions that should be addressed.

I do want to remind you that what we are talking about here are the very early stages of a company coming into existence. This is essentially the point when a group of friends have made something useful, and now it's time to take it seriously.

When should the company form?

In its simplest terms, you should form the company as soon as money will be involved. This could mean that there are investors who are putting money into the company. It could also mean that you have a product that has started making money.

If this was the case you could file a company very early around one idea. Then, why do you need all the rest of this process? Filing a company is simple, and at around $300 for an LLC, why not just get on with it?

The answer is, because you are going to have to change it while it is underway. You'll never get the percentages quite right upfront. You also can't be 100% sure of the team's commitment levels until you get down to brass tacks. The the longer you delay your filing, the more accurately you can map the company filed on paper to what the real company is. If you file too early, you are ignoring how little you understand about your team and idea.

There's a downside to filing later, however: If you file late, it's hard to manage emotional and tax issues implied with involving money.

Again, It boils down to trust. The team needs some degree of trust if you are going to delay. If they don't have it, then your hand is forced, and you'll need to file the company or lose your team. So this will hinge on your leadership skills to convince your team that it's best to postpone the filing.

If you do have to file the company early in the process, make sure to plan a meeting later to refile the company based on the performance of the team and any investment that was issued along the way. I described this earlier in the book as an *annealing meeting*. It gives all the tensions built up over the creation of the company a chance to be relaxed.

Thus with this strategy you will have created a company, but more as a kind of placeholder, with the intention of adjusting it later.

Who is responsible for the company?

Forming a Team of Three
I mentioned above that you should wait until money is going to be involved in the company before you file it. The reason was that corporate structures this early are primarily to figure out who owes taxes on what. What this will do is force the ownership question to be answered. But if you have been using the charter, tracking debt, and created an ownership structure already, then this step should be procedural.

Filing also forces another question: Who is going to be doing what role in the company? This implies a corporate structure and for some people to be given titles. With those titles come responsibility. Strangely, you can call yourselves anything you want, make silly business cards, and get credit cards with your title listed as "Champion of Finance".

Yes, at an early stage it is somewhat funny to ask your only co-founder, "Who wants to be president?" To you, the company is so small, and there is so much to do before this matters, that it really is pointless. While you are executing on the charter everyone already knows their jobs and what expectations are for them. But if you are actually operating a company then you are going to get frustrated if nuts-and-bolts tasks don't get completed because your team members are unsure who has responsibility for them. For example, whose job is it to move money to the IRS every month so you can pay your corporate taxes every quarter? Whose job was it to find new people; what about managing the company image?

Let's examine titles in a bit more detail.

When should you have titles?

If possible, start executing on the charter and wait until the last possible moment to file the company. When you file the company, award the following three titles, CEO, COO, and CFO.

Let the group work out the arrangement of roles, then award the positions. You probably already know who among your team should fill which role, but let the process unfold on its own. The natural person for each position will be obvious to all by the time you have to involve money.

What titles should your organization have?

I believe the the following titles must be figured out early on; everything else can be figured out later. When money and responsibility are involved, however, there are certain implied expectations that need to be met.

CEO
This is the person focused on strategic long-term decisions. He or she typically holds a position on the board. His role is to be the keeper of the vision for the company, and as such, he should be passionate about it. He is also most likely to be the person selling the product and vision. It will be this person whose job it is to keep everyone thinking about the bigger picture.

COO
Someone has to actually keep the business operating and is sometimes called the President. That is the role of the Chief Operations Officer. When you are past the creating stage and into running the company you need someone to step up and keep the place running from day to day. He or she will be focused on tactical day-to-day operations.

CFO
Someone needs to deal with money. He or she should be dealing with purchasing, payroll, taxes, and generally figuring out if the company is even moving forward. She needs to be good at this subject and enjoy things being organized and timely.

Why this trio?
If people are assigned these three roles, then they can argue and talk out issues that are necessary for making an effective company. For instance, whoever is the CFO argues for budget and makes the others keep their minds on money. Whoever is the COO argues for more resources to accomplish the existing tasks and projects. Finally, the CEO argues for moving the company into better strategic market positions. So the COO and CEO are both looking for new resources and the CFO has to keep everyone realistic about what is possible.

This trio is a great arrangement, really, because it forces the core of the business to be discussed regularly. The problem is that if any one person has to do two or more of these roles, that person must internalize all of these decisions. It helps to get the discussions out in the open and to get accustomed to proposing solutions and working as a team.

Why is the CTO not included?

The CTO is the person who is focused on the technology of the company. In terms of software startups, they are usually the person who wrote the code originally. Later, this will be the person who must argue the budget and the development decisions.

This is a very important role, however when you strip a business down to it's essentials this is an extension of the role of COO. If you can easily separate operations from the technology used to enable it, then you should have a 4th role of CTO. For the sake of starting a company, make sure you have a COO and let that person suggest their CTO.

Should you use titles as rewards?

Do not give everyone a title to make them all feel equal. If you are founding a company of programmers, everyone wants to be the CTO. But in an early-stage tech company, you don't really need someone making high-level technology decisions. The team can decide that together. All creating a CTO role would do is create conflict and resentment that someone is now "in charge." Titles are not an effective way of aligning a team. They are a way to help your team members each focus on one area of the business so that they do not have to focus on all areas of the business.

How do you match them up?

Regarding team roles, earlier on I advocated the roles of *Visionary*, *Leader*, and *Members* for the team. But, at this later stage I am talking about *CEO*, *COO*, and *CFO*. The question becomes, how do you map from one group to the other?

It would be nice to say that the Visionary becomes the CEO, the Leader becomes the COO, and somewhere a CFO appears. But, this often isn't going to be the case.

Where did the Visionary go? It is very possible that the Visionary who originally started the company moved on to create new visions. If he liked the idea and got the ball rolling this might be all that he had been looking to accomplish.

However in the course of building the product and operating it you should have an obvious CEO, COO, and CFO. Odds are they would be contributing the most to the company and as a result own most of the company already. So by the time you get to filing the company, these roles should already be filled.

If you do not find the right people, then after the company is running you should actively look for someone to fill these roles. These people might be on the existing team or they might come from outside of the team.

What should each person be responsible for?

Let me reiterate that this is very early-stage role definition. As the company grows, any of these roles might branch off and these responsibilities delegated to other people. The tasks involved in each role might be outsourced, but someone who has a stake in the company must represent these views.

I find the split to be conveniently between the *dream*, *resources*, and *money*. So even if you do not agree with the list of responsibilities, look at the core as to what each of these people must embody.

CEO (Dream)

- Represents forces outside the organization
- Focused on sales
- Keeper of the dream
- Sets vision and direction (based on listening to everyone else

and teasing out common goals)

- Recruits people to the company.
- Very people-centric
- Keeps everyone together as a team

COO (Resources)

- Represents forces inside the organization
- Focused on delivering the product or service
- Head of all project managers
- Sets policy for running projects
- Constantly optimizing to improve quality, cost, and delivery time.
- Responsible for resources, space, materials, and labor for creating and delivering the product.

CFO (Money)

- Represents the cost of reality
- Responsible for tracking how the company is doing.
- Works with the CEO to set attainable targets
- Works with the COO to track utilization
- Handles purchasing
- Handles billing
- Advising on raises/ salaries/ bonuses

When should they be responsible for something?

All of these roles are required at some level, but they are not required constantly. There are more practical day-to-day roles that must be filled - notably, the constant grind of selling and delivering on those sales. But occasionally everyone needs to put on their C-level hat and talk. On a monthly, quarterly, and yearly basis you should meet and review the following topics:

CEO

- Reflect on the sales that were made, the customers maintained, and how the world has changed

- Propose large changes for the company

- Relate what he has learned listening to the company and clients.

COO

- Review how sales were fulfilled and propose new optimizations

- Review how resources could have been better procured.

CFO

- Review last year's targets versus what actually was accomplished

- Propose Salary changes and increases in bonuses

Chapter 15: Goodbye!

In the course of writing this book, my thoughts on ideas have changed. I had always found joy in coming up with fun ideas and pitching them to people for the sake of amusement. These ideas had never meant much to me; they were just fun. They got people to talk and to enjoy the conversation. I think somewhere along the way, though, I got more interested in the fact that I could come up with these ideas in the first place. I started collecting my ideas on paper, and pretty soon I had hundreds of them.

The problem was that these ideas never went anywhere. Perhaps, I thought, I could research them in more detail, but the only thing I was checking for was "has someone done this already?" I would have validation that a particular idea was a good one only after learning that someone else actually brought it to fruition.

After writing this book, my thoughts have changed a bit. It isn't so important to find that one- or two-line idea that ties everything together. Sure, there are places for this sort of cleverness, but searching for the idea is not what is most important; it's the *people* who join you to look for the idea and *where* you are looking for the idea that really matter.

Finding the perfect idea is a myth. I don't think there is a Platonic idea out there that once uncovered will give you an advantage to creating it. It's the journey that matters. If you plan on having others join you, you must point out where you are going so that the idea becomes more of a destination on the horizon than an actual goal. By the time you get to your first goal, you will see something even greater just a little farther off.

It is this paradox that I have been working on for a long time. How can something so insignificant as an idea also be the single most defining step of something that can encompass a lifetime? Without that initial idea, you wouldn't have empires or nations. Isolated, they are almost useless; but the right idea at just the right moment, with just the right team behind it, is possibly the most powerful force that human beings can bring forth.

I have sought to put together a process and to generalize what my group is doing into a very natural set of steps. I hope when you read this book it all appears self-evident. That would represent success for me. What I have left out are all of the failures, experiments, and projects that got me to this point. I have many stories that would show how some aspect of this process was ignored and caused problems as a result later on.

Let me leave you with this thought: Ideas are leadership tools. Ideas are ideals, but most importantly, ideas are shared thoughts. For me to explain my idea you must think like me. In doing so you cannot understand my idea without having a copy of it and thus I lose control of it. Most of the drama of business lies in this question of who thought of something first and how much they deserve for coming up with this idea. In the end, though, the merit of the idea is not who originated it but how well it can be used to motivate and inspire your team.

Focus on your team. Focus on problems that interest you. The ideas will follow.

Good luck!

Acknowledgements

- ➢ Neil Johnson for telling me to write my ideas down and helping to make this book readable.

- ➢ Kevin Klinemeier for telling me to write a book.

- ➢ Ryan Smits for co-founding endless companies together.

- ➢ Isaac Nichols for exploring what it takes to turn a Vision into a Company.

- ➢ Adam Hindman for the endless talks about these matters when getting coffee.

- John Secrest for his method of looking for ideas around problems, demographics and technology.

- Joe Justice for his insight on leadership and being a visionary.

- Scott White for his ideas on the bootstrapping a company.

About the Author

Matt Paulin lives and works in Seattle. He has been involved in numerous startups, collaborations, and software products. He has degree in Electrical Engineering from Kansas State University, and has spend several decades doing software development. This is his first book.

Further Reading

"Applied imagination". Osborn, Alex F. Oxford, England: Scribner'S. (1953).

"The brainstorming myth" by Jonah Lehrer, New Yorker Magazine: January 30, 2012

"The Lean Startup" by Eric Ries (2011)

"Gamestorming" by Dave Gray, Sunni Brown, and James Macanufo (2010)

www.ingramcontent.com/pod-product-compliance
Lightning Source LLC
Chambersburg PA
CBHW051803170526
45167CB00005B/1862